D0113794

AUDIO
SWEETENING
FOR
FILM AND TV

**MILTON C. HUBATKA, FREDERICK HULL,
AND RICHARD W. SANDERS**

Editor: Vincent L. Wolfe

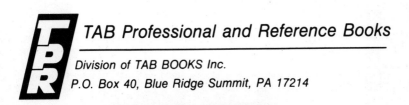

TAB *Professional and Reference Books*

Division of TAB BOOKS Inc.
P.O. Box 40, Blue Ridge Summit, PA 17214

MERCYHURST COLLEGE
HAMMERMILL LIBRARY
ERIE, PA. 16546

On March 28, 1985, two weeks after completing this book, Milton Hubatka passed on to new dimensions.

FIRST EDITION

FIRST PRINTING

Copyright © 1985 by TAB BOOKS Inc.

Printed in the United States of America

Reproduction or publication of the content in any manner, without express permission of the publisher, is prohibited. No liability is assumed with respect to the use of the information herein.

Library of Congress Cataloging in Publication Data

Hubatka, Milton C.
   Audio sweetening for film and TV.

   Includes index.
   1. Moving-pictures, Talking. 2. Dubbing of moving-pictures. I. Hull, Frederick. II. Sanders, Richard W.
III. Title.
TR897.H83 1985   778.5'2344   85-22257
ISBN 0-8306-1994-1

Front cover photograph courtesy of Mobile Audio, National City Bank Building, P.O. Box 6115, Rome, GA 30161.

Contents

Acknowledgment

The authors express their gratitude to the following people for their contributions to the development of this book:

Judy Elsen
David Johansen
David Oren
Jim Lucas
Harry Adams
David Davis
Soren Bredsdorff
Vince Bassie
Michael Zinberg
John Pratt
Shoni Ogier
Cliff Fenneman
Steve Long
Joe Garguilo
Vicki Hart
Mutia Hull
Al McPherson
George Lydecker

and Tajie, who had the best ears of all.

Introduction

sweet • en \'swēt-ən\ *vt* **1** : to make something more pleasing to the senses **2** : to increase the agreeable qualities **3** : to add elements to an audio track during the postproduction process to improve the quality (production value) of the program

Technology has played an all-important role in the production of television programs for entertainment, industrial communications, and education. In the same way technology has brought the personal computer within the reach of most business and professional people, video production equipment has fallen in price and increased in quality proportionately. Virtually anyone can now rent a high-quality, industrial-grade camera and video tape recorder (VTR) and produce acceptable picture quality. Differentiating among producers of such material then becomes a matter of evaluating their communication or entertainment capabilities and talent, enhanced by other elements that contribute to the production value of a program. The quality of the sound track accompanying the video portion of the program is one facet of the production process that allows some producers to stand apart from the others.

Sweetening audio tracks for productions on a smaller scale (defined as industrials, educationals, cable TV programs, or low-budget TV commercials) has become cost-effective only in the past few years, with the introduction of high-quality, intelligent multitrack recorders costing approximately $6000 for eight tracks, combined with lost-cost, high-quality mixing consoles and microprocessor-based synchronizers capable of interlocking a VTR and multitrack audio tape recorder (ATR) via SMPTE time code, in absolute synchronization. Were this equipment not as cost-effective as video production equipment itself, the producer would not have the capability to create sophisticated sound tracks on small budgets.

Sweetening an audio track allows the producer to draw from a wide range of sources both creative and technical, using hardware and software to fix, supplement, and mix audio tracks for video and other visual media. Since the days of the "talkies," movies have had sound tracks built and mixed. This process is called *dubbing* in film and *audio sweetening* in tape. Both refer to producing sound tracks.

Sweetening provides the viewer much more sensory stimulation. Many believe a good sound track can save a mediocre program, but good visuals can't save a bad track. Sweetening increases the level of suggestion and impression of the visual medium. As you will learn in Chapter 8, a variety of background presence or ambient sound allows you to place a scene anywhere. For example, introducing a background presence loop to an airport shot on a sound stage or set can move it to any locale, either domestic or foreign, through effective placement of public-address pages, etc.

The authors building a sound track for a video tape industrial program at their small-scale audio sweetening bay in Boulder, Colorado.

Sweetening gives the producer the ability to draw from many sources of sounds to create an image or impression. The producer can make or buy sound effects (SFX) and background presence. Sweetening allows a producer much more control over moods and perceptions, beyond simple music selection. Sweetening provides the opportunity to fix poorly recorded production audio by various means, such as equalization or the process of separating or totally replacing dialog or other on-camera audio.

Affordable multitrack audio tape recorders (ATRs) such as the TASCAM 44 have been available since the mid-1970s (courtesy TASCAM).

Low-cost synchronizers, making possible the audio-video interlock, did not become available until the early 1980s.

The audio equipment necessary to sweeten video has been available since the mid-1970s. Companies such as TASCAM (Teac Corporation of America's professional products group) and Otari have been producing low-cost, multitrack audio recorders and mixing consoles to meet the demand of musicians who wish to produce recordings on a smaller scale than that enjoyed by artists with record label backing. The microprocessor also has been available since the mid-1970s, but it took several years for this technology to filter down and become sufficiently cost-effective for control applications such as synchronizers. It is the merging of these technologies that has brought audio sweetening within the reach of producers of small-scale productions.

Outside of Hollywood, Chicago, and New York, few post-production facilities have audio sweetening facilities. Recently, however, technically aware producers, both independent and corporate, have begun installing the equipment necessary to interface multitrack ATRs and video tape recorders. Such a facility has been integrated at The Visual Communications Group, Inc., two principals of which are the coauthors of this book. The Visual Communications Group produces a wide range of industrial, corporate communications, educational, and cable TV entertainment programs, as well as multi-image presentations and low-budget TV spots—all of which are sweetened using equipment and techniques illustrated in this book.

Why Sweeten?

Sophisticated audiences demand high-quality productions, from both a video and audio standpoint. Network television programs set the standard for the viewer's perception of production quality. Video tape tends to be a rather unforgiving medium to the inexperienced producer: every viewer is an expert on quality because of the amount of material he or she has had as a reference. If you expect to produce for visual media, audio sweetening is an integral part of the production process.

Dialog and narration, music and sound effects, used in careful combination, enhance not just the quality but the communicative ability of visual images. Sound can help clarify visuals and change or expand their meaning, making them realistic or symbolic, objective or subjective. Sound can range from great exaggeration and distortion to sparse isolation to silence. It can be contrasted against visuals as well as synchronized with them, or employed in transi-

A Hollywood-scale sweetening bay such as this one at Glen Glenn Sound represents millions of dollars worth of equipment.

Music, narration, on-camera dialog, and sound effects are the software elements of the sweetening process.

tions. It can even be synthesized to express new or unusual moods and effects.

Technology has made sweetening cost-effective and put it within reach of nearly all producers. Various levels of financial capability and artistic and technical expertise can be reached as well. The technique is simple and can be employed by any producer with minimal technical awareness. With the capabilities of electronic video tape editors (both control track and computerized) utilizing time code, and some basic multitrack audio equipment with a low-cost synchronizer—plus technique, ideas, and knowledge of the medium—anyone who has the desire to do so can build great audio tracks. Audio tracks can be built that provide better communication and increase the power of the visual medium.

Movies like *Star Wars* have served to elevate public awareness of great sound tracks, as have MTV, stereo hi-fi, video cassettes, and cable TV. Technology is growing fast, and producers should take advantage of it. "Chops don't come in box," a phrase we believe was coined by someone at TASCAM, is very appropriate to audio sweetening. Musicians call practicing and perfecting their technique and their art "keeping their chops up." You can't buy those chops; they come only with many hours of practice and experimentation.

To get your "chops" for audio sweetening, you must experiment and practice.

Producers of programmed multi-image presentations would not consider producing a program without sophisticated sound tracks produced on multitrack ATRs, requiring the mixing of music, narration, dialog, sound effects, and background presence. The state of the art in multi-image has included such sound tracks for years. This technology and capability has become available to producers using video tape as the production medium only in the past few years. The primary reason for this has been recent cost reductions both of synchronizers to interlock the VTR and multitrack ATR, and the logic design incorporated into low-cost, multitrack ATRs that makes this synchronization possible. The multitrack machine must have the electronic capability to control the speed and logic functions, and to be controlled by an external device.

This Book

This book will introduce the necessary concepts, artistic considerations, techniques, and processes (both basic and advanced) for sweetening, as well as provide a review of the hardware elements necessary for various levels of audio sweetening. It will explain how to apply various proven techniques to new areas of communication, information, and entertainment media. It also will introduce the role and discuss the impact of computers and other new innovations like optical and compact disks, hi-fi and stereo video cassettes, and stereo television.

The book begins with a brief history of sweetening as it evolved in the Hollywood production environment. The following chapter presents a generalized overview of the whole sweetening process, building a framework for the practical considerations that follow. Some fundamentals of audio recording are discussed, since good recording makes sweetening easier. Video editing typically precedes sweetening, so it is addressed next, emphasizing editing audio and the relationship to postedit sweetening. The basic hardware or "tools of the trade," specifically those tools that relate to system control and synchronization, are the next topic. Audio hardware is a vast field, lightly touched in Chapter 6. Chapter 7 presents varieties of system configurations and how they affect the practical operations. The sweetening techniques chapter includes assorted practical advice on dealing with some of the software elements of the sweetening process. Related to techniques but worthy of a whole chapter is music selection, production, and integration. Chapter 10 discusses sweetening facilities, and the final chapter looks at the future of small-scale audio sweetening.

The three authors bring a variety of knowledge into the brewing of this book. Milton C. Hubatka was a producer and director who learned the processes in Hollywood. Fred Hull provides engineering background and recent production experience to integrate the processes into the industrial, educational, and cable TV environment. As a composer, music producer, and audio engineer, Richard Sanders contributes audio expertise on both the technical and aesthetic fronts. The writing assignments were divided among the three according to individual experience, so you may notice several writing styles. Rather than edit the material to merge the individual styles, the authors elected to keep the styles distinct in the various sections of the book.

This book is an introduction, not a bible of sweetening. An individual's tastes and personal perceptions of techniques will prevail. The subject matter requires that anyone who wishes to learn the techniques of audio sweetening must first learn the basics, similar to learning the basic techniques of video or film production. Once these are mastered, however, only one's creativity and perseverance can limit the results.

Once exposed to the basics of audio sweetening, the producer or director will never again "listen" to a production normally. In a way parallel to how we all view media material in general, always dissecting every shot or scene, we will apply the same critical ear to the audio portion of productions, regardless of whether we are viewing TV spots, industrials, TV programs, or feature films. Producers, directors, and other creative types continually review new material, study the style and techniques of others, and then incorporate the best into their own style. Just as we have done this with the "look" of our material, we now have the opportunity to incorporate sound into our own styles.

Chapter 1

The History
of Audio Sweetening

---

dub • bing \\'dəb-iŋ \\ *n*　**1**　: the process of recreating,
adding sound effects and music, and then remixing
discrete elements to one or more tracks of a film　**2**　:
in video, the process of making copies of a video tape.
To avoid confusion, *audio sweetening* is the video term
for *sound dubbing*.

The early 1900s brought the silent picture, "the golden age of the
silent cinema." Music (typically the piano or organ) accompanied
the pictures, played by a musician at the base of the screen. International distribution of films was never a problem because of
language barriers during the silent picture era.

A motion picture entitled *The Jazz Singer* is credited as having
the first sound track, in 1927. Optical sound tracks didn't become
a reality until 1928 and 1929, giving motion pictures authenticity
and the ability to reenact real life. Synchronized sound, however,
took its toll on certain silent film stars whose voices didn't quite
match their on-screen images. It also introduced a new problem
to be dealt with, language barriers, which complicated foreign
distribution and led to the practice of subtitling.

World War II brought new applications for the cinema, with
newsreels detailing the military efforts abroad; then the turn of the
decade brought television. During the 1960s, larger screen formats

such as 70 mm required the adaptation of magnetic tape technology to film, replacing the optical sound tracks with multiple magnetic stripes carrying stereo sound for pictures such as *Around The World in 80 Days* (Fig. 1-1).

Outside the film world, in 1941 Leslie Polfuss (better known as Les Paul) had the idea of recording several guitar parts, one on top of another. By 1948 (with the release of "Lover") the idea had become a commercial success, and in 1954 Les Paul built the first 8-track recorder. At this time the rest of the recording industry was still using mono machines, recording background tracks on one machine and then transferring them to a second machine while adding vocals. Today only one stereo machine is required for this process, known as *sound-on-sound*. When the first stereo albums were released in 1958, 2- and 3-track recorders were still the industry standard. By the early 1960s, 4-track had arrived, and by the end of the decade, 8-track was becoming the standard recording format (Fig. 1-2).

It was the recording industry of the 1960s that created the requirement and spurred the development of the multitrack audio tape recorder (ATR). During the last 1960s and early 1970s, com-

Fig. 1-1. Film dubbing differs from audio sweetening only in that the source material for sound effects, music, dialog, etc., is recorded and interlocked on magnetic film with sprocket holes instead of multitrack magnetic audio tape with time code. Pictured here are dubbing units at Glen Glenn Sound.

Fig. 1-2. One of the earliest multitrack ATRs was the Ampex 448, an 8-track, 1″ machine on which many a hit single was recorded, but which was little used for audio sweetening.

puterized editing equipment allowed video tape to become a much more attractive and cost-effective production medium. Time coding allowed frame-accurate synchronization, and in 1969 the Society of Motion Picture and Television Engineers (SMPTE) formally adopted a standard for a time code of HR:MN:SC:FR—hours, minutes, seconds, and frames.

Although video tape had been used for "live-cut" shows during the 1960s, little actual editing was done until the early 1970s. When editing became possible, programs recorded with live audiences found that they needed to have their audio "fixed" because tape editing cut off applause, laughter, and other "live" sounds. Variety shows and situation comedies ("sitcoms") were particularly vulnerable to this problem, thus becoming the first applications of computerized video tape editing to entertainment programs.

What was required was a process that would allow post-processing of the audio track of the program. Situation comedies such as "I Love Lucy," although shot and posted on film, required "fixing" of the sound tracks, chiefly bridging the live audience's laughs, which had been chopped off by editing. Charlie Douglas formed a company named Northridge Electronics to make several portable "laugh machines," which used mechanical drive systems to actuate the laughs and applause, on cue, from a typewriter-like keyboard. As the sitcoms increased in popularity and required more and more laugh men two other men, John and Carrol Pratt, also worked with Charlie Douglas, using clones of his machine. Coauthor Milton Hubatka was first introduced to the process of audio sweetening on video tape while working with John Pratt on the Mary Tyler Moore and Bob Newhart shows.

As the transition from three-camera film to 2″ video tape for network sitcoms took place (due primarily to the advent of the CMX video tape editing system), more and more sitcoms were produced on tape; all of Norman Lear's shows, from "*All In the Family*" onward, were produced on tape. Once video tape could be edited, the sitcom was the ideal vehicle for video production. Audio postproduction was still a problem.

In the mid-1970s two organizations were devising ways to convert the traditional film-dubbing methods to video tape. Vidtronics was primarily a video tape postproduction facility, while Glen Glenn Sound was chiefly a film-dubbing house. Both had clients who needed sound track fixing for video taped shows, "Hee Haw" at Vidtronics and "The Bill Cosby Show" at Glen Glenn. Both started research and development simultaneously, both using the same basic hardware: Scully 4-track ATRs, with EECO editors controlled by a series of proprietary and mysterious "black boxes." Glen Glenn Sound called their system PAP, for "post audio processing," and it is still in use (Fig. 1-3).

The techniques that both firms were using had been more or less borrowed from film-dubbing practice, and their synchroniza-

4

Fig. 1-3. One of the early PAP (post audio production) systems developed at Glen Glenn Sound. Source material was transferred from 1/4″ tape and NAB cartridges to 16-track Ampex MM-1100s.

Fig. 1-4. The Glen Glenn PAP system is still being used today; although the system has become very computerized, it still uses the Ampex MM-1100.

tion technology fell far short of modern microprocessor capabilities (though Intel had introduced a microprocessor at about this same time). The recording industry was spawning more complex multitrack recorders such as the Ampex MM1100, which Glen Glenn still uses (Fig. 1-4). Then, late in the 1970s, synchronizers such as those manufactured by Adams-Smith and BTX (now Cipher Digital) began to replace the proprietary black boxes—but still only large-scale production facilities like Vidtronics, Glen Glenn, and the major studios could afford them.

In the early 1980s, almost a decade later, application of microprocessor technology has brought the cost of all equipment down to where it is appropriate for small productions and small budgets. During the early 1980's synchronizers, intelligent multitracks, and cooperative design efforts between various manufacturers provided the industry with compatibility.

We at The Visual Communications Group, Inc., having been involved with the technology and techniques from their inception, have adapted the process and utilized new, cost-effective technology to provide the same capability for smaller-scale productions that until recently was available only at major production facilities. the difference between "Hollywood" or large-scale audio sweetening and the sweetening described in this book is merely that of equipment cost; the process is identical.

Chapter 2

The Sweetening Process

---

pro • cess \ 'präs-es \ *n* **1** : a succession of actions
taken to bring about some desired result **2** : the tried-
and-true manner of sweetening a video program

As in many aspects of production, regardless of the medium, a
"tried and true" sweetening process has evolved in the television
business. As executed on the Hollywood scale, the process grew
out of the film industry and conceptually follows the steps and conventions used in creating sound tracks for films. Practically, the
physical techniques are dependent on the medium and the hardware, and therein lie the differences from film techniques. The complete process breaks down logically into six distinct subtasks; any
individual sweetening job may include all or only some of these
steps.

This chapter provides a functional overview of the process broken down into six steps. These steps and the order they are
presented are representative of a typical sweetening job on a full-
scale, Hollywood-type video production. For smaller-scale productions, the functions of the six steps are similar, but the sequence
of execution may vary depending on specific production requirements, on the postproduction environment and methods, and
on the preferences of the producers.

In the Hollywood method, most of the sweetening is performed after the final video edit is completed. During the video edit, the principal dialog tracks and perhaps synchronized music are recorded to the *edit master* (EM) along with the picture; these audio tracks may be final or used only for reference in sweetening. Once the video edit is completed, the video edit bay is freed and concentration turns to audio.

This method has evolved in Hollywood because, typically, the on-line mastering room (bay) for the video portion of a program is separated from the audio sweetening bay. The principal reason for the separation is economic. If a full complement of audio sweetening equipment were included in a 1″ video edit bay, then the 24-track ATR(s) and mixing console would be relatively idle while the operations focused on video editing; conversely, several 1″ VTRs and the video switcher would be relatively idle during audio processing. In a high-volume production environment, these expensive pieces of equipment must be utilized to maximum efficiency. By separating the audio and video portions of the posting process, the productivity of the high-dollar equipment increases markedly.

This may or may not be true in the case of small-scale sweetening bays, where it may not be practical to separate the functions due to the necessary "overhead" equipment. Addition of sweetening to an existing video edit bay requires the purchase of hardware specific to the sweetening process, while utilizing much of the other equipment already in place. Adding a separate sweetening bay requires purchase of one or more additional VTRs, video monitors, and time code equipment that are already present in the video edit bay. Hence it would be more common in the small-scale environment to find an integrated video editing and audio sweetening bay.

The integrated video/audio bay allows variations in the sequence of execution of the steps in the sweetening process. Rather than saving the audio process until the video edit is completed, it may be more efficient to build portions of the audio in parallel with the video. In fact, if the video edit system uses a control track edit controller, certain parts of the audio *must* be built in parallel with the video to maintain exact sync. But more on that later. The point is that the following breakdown of the sweetening process into steps describes the Hollywood style and is applicable to the small-scale environment in general—but it must be molded to the individual needs and resources of a particular project or company.

SPOTTING

The first step in the sweetening process is planning the soundtrack. While much of the soundtrack is dictated by the script and the recorded action, much remains to be added, enhanced, or modified in the post process. Analyzing the edited video program and planning for each element of the final audio track is called *spotting*. Spotting determines what is needed where in terms of music cues, sound effects, background presence, dialog replacement, narration, etc.

When sweetening Hollywood-scale TV shows, the spotting session is often a grand affair hosted by the producer or associate producer. The sound effects, dialog, and music editors usually attend, accompanied by the composer and his or her entourage. When sweetening small-scale productions, without union or other similar constraints, the task is a lonely one, usually delegated to the producer or director. Spotting is mostly a tedious task but it does require experience and creativity, for careful selection and timely placement of music and effects can have a powerful impact in a program.

The first thing needed for the spotting session is a dub of the edited master (EM) with time code numbers inserted in the picture. Given the fact that the show is in its final edited form, a dub with time code numbers on the screen will match the finished program exactly. The time code, inserted on the screen with a character inserter, *should* be identical to that of the edited master. This will save a lot of headaches in calculating offsets. Some people prefer to make the time code window very large, occupying a large portion of the screen. Make your time code window whatever size is most comfortable for you. The picture area doesn't really matter at this point because all video editing has already been accomplished. You may wish to make the numbers very large, depending on how far your monitor is placed from the mixing console.

The producer, director, or other technically able person views a dub with SMPTE time code and notes cues for music, narration, dialog, and sound effects (Fig. 2-1). A formalized spotting sheet be very helpful. Figure 2-2 is a suggested model for a spotting sheet, but you should consider customizing the sheet as your experience and preferences dictate. It is best to use a VTR with forward and reverse "search or shuttle" capability to find cue points accurately. Spotting isn't something that you can typically do "on-the-fly," so having a machine that can back up and go forward at frame-by-frame rates, finding the exact frame for the cue, is almost a necessity. Once you have found the desired frame number, note it on the spotting sheet. At this time, it is a good idea to make track assignments, identifying on which track of the multitrack ATR the cue should be placed.

Fig. 2-1. The producer or other technically able person views a dub of the show recorded with a time code window and notes, on a spotting form, where music, sound effects, narration, etc., should start and end.

There are two different ways to spot a show, one being to start at the top of the show and work through it scene-by-scene, noting each cue, music, sound effects, narration, etc., as it occurs. Another method is to work through the show, starting at the top, but only noting one type of cue (music cues, for example) from beginning to end, then starting over and noting only, say, sound effects cues. Then you would rewind, start from the top, and on the next pass note only narration cues. You would repeat this process, starting from the beginning of the show and working through, element by element, until the entire show is spotted for each element. Either method of spotting is adequate and it is up to one's personal choice to use whatever method or combination works the best.

While spotting, you should also make track assignments, deciding which effect or cue should be placed on which channel of the multitrack audio tape recorder, especially if you have a limited number of tracks available. This saves time during the track-

10

VIDEO/AUDIO SWEETENING SPOTTING SHEET

SHOW TITLE: ITVA DEMO
PROD. No

TRACK ASSIGNMENTS

DATE: 27 MARCH

TIME CODE CUE	VIDEO	SOUND EFFECT	NOTES	1	2	3	4	5	6	7	8	MIX HOLD CODE
00:00		PRODUCTION TRACK		X →								
00:00	00:10 OUT	INTRO MUSIC CUE				X						
00:00		BACK GROUND MUSIC			X							
00:11:00		DOOR OPEN				X						
00:14:00		DOOR CLOSE				X						
00:14:18		GLASSCRASH					X					
18:25 27:22		FLYBY						X →				
31:23		CAR DOOR OPEN			X →	X →						
35:08		CAR DOOR CLOSE										
36:13		ENGINE START & TIRE SQUEAL			X →							
38:08		TIRE SCREECH			X →	X						
45:16		ENDING MUSIC CUE										

Fig. 2-2. A typical spotting form.

building process and provides for greater overall organization of the process. Making these track assignments during the spotting session also assures that you are not assigning multiple cues or effects to the same track, thus erasing a previously recorded element. If you are working with limited tracks, the availability of open tracks may affect the plan for the soundtrack. For example, a subtle sound effect behind narration and music might be a nice touch, but if there is no open track, that idea might be sacrificed to avoid a submix. A question then arises. If that effect is omitted here, should it be included elsewhere in the program or omitted for consistency? As such, planning the track usage is an important part of the spotting process.

During spotting it can be useful to face the real but unfortunate issue of fixing problems—problems either in field recording or in the edited master. Ideally there are no problems in original recording or in the editing of audio tracks onto the EM, but fixing problems is an inevitable part of real-world sweetening. During spotting, careful attention to the audio on the edited master will identify problems that must be fixed in the track-building phase. If the audio on the EM is only a "scratch track," it should be examined for problems in the original recordings which will need special attention when the actual tracks are built on the ATR. If the audio on the EM is to be laid down and used in the final mix, it must be spotted for recording imperfections, plus level or tone changes at edit points and gaps in background presence, that are problems induced in the edit.

The product of the spotting session is a list, resembling an edit decision list, which has all of the audio events listed in order. This list is used to build the tracks, and can also be used as the "cue sheet" or sweetening log by the mixing engineer or producer. A personal computer can often make spotting cues more efficient (Fig. 2-3).

This spotting session, as described, fits into postproduction after the video edit is completed. In some postproduction situations, audio tracks will be built on the ATR in parallel with the video edit. In this case, the cues are either fully planned ahead or spotted individually during the video edit. A spotting session will still be useful after the edit to determine further additions or alterations to the tracks, post-edit.

GATHERING AND PREPARING MATERIALS

The next step after spotting is to select and prepare the required source materials, i.e., music cues, sound effects, narration, and dialog pickups, if necessary. Building sound tracks usually re-

Fig. 2-3. A personal computer may make a spotting session more efficient. Here the monitor is switch-selectable between the VTR and the computer. Milt Hubatka listens to a potential music cue behind narration.

quires a great variety of source materials which are rarely all available in one place and often must be recorded or edited or manufactured prior to the track-building process. Recording narration, in or out of house, previewing and selecting music and effects from various libraries, and creating effects and ambience loops all take time and leg work. Gathering and preparing these materials before entering the sweetening bay will reap tremendous savings in studio time. As in all other processes in the production of a program, planning, organization, and preparation save time and money later. In sweetening, the first two steps, spotting and gathering materials, are accomplished without the use of a lot of expensive equipment that shouldn't be unnecessarily tied up. This is especially important if you sweeten in a commercial facility charging by the hour, or if your in-house sweetening equipment is in heavy demand. In either case, prepared source materials will minimize the actual time in the bay.

If you are using your own sweetening bay, you know what equipment and materials you have available. On the other hand, if you must go to an outside facility you may be disappointed with the materials available for your use. Some sweetening houses have extensive libraries of sound effects and music cues on NAB (National Association of Broadcasters) cartridges that are easily dropped into a show. Other houses have very small libraries that are limited to presence that won't match your scenes, sound effects that include only train whistles, sirens, animal grunts, or the first 12 volumes of the Network music library.

The best advice is to bring your own materials—complete. Unless you know the library of your sweetening house very well, you will be better off gathering your materials at the rate of $50 or so per hour, from a studio that specializes in music and effects, rather than paying the $100 or $200 hourly rate of the sweetening bay while you select material.

If you are sweetening at an outside facility, it is good practice to consult both your sweetening facility and the studio from which you plan to select your materials, verifying compatibility prior to any postproduction activities. Sometimes it is advisable to time code all of your source material (on the vacant track of a 1/4″ 2-track or 1/2″ 4-track machine) to lock-up with the multitrack for long, precise music or narration cues.

Dialog should be the source element requiring least preparation. With luck, all of the production dialog tracks are intact on the edited video master. It might be necessary, however, to pull material from video masters to fill holes or to make small corrections. Locating the required video field masters is a simple task.

Natural effects and ambience also come from the video field masters, but occasionally these will be easier to use in another format. Presence loops are the best example; creating a presence loop can save significant time in later phases of sweetening (Fig. 2-4). Fabricating these loops will be discussed later.

Recording narration is familiar to all video producers. Whether used as the sole audio element in a simple video edit or as one element of a sweetened track, properly recorded narration is essential. To prepare for sweetening, determine the best medium for the recording session. After recording, a razor blade edit of the narration either in the audio studio or in your office is usually more economical than locating the good takes in the video or the sweetening room.

Libraries are the principal source for music cues and sound effects. The preparation begins by previewing and selecting cues to fit the requirements identified in the spotting session. These cues often must be transferred from the distribution format to another medium, either for transportation or compatibility. The libraries are most often available on phonograph record; the most convenient medium for the sweetening bay, however, may be mono or stereo 1/4″ audio tape, (full-track or 2-track), 1/2″ 4-track audio

Fig. 2-4. The source materials come from field master video cassettes, 1/4″ audio tape reels, record albums, and possibly audio cassettes. It is necessary to gather all materials prior to the next step in the sweetening process.

tape, audio or video cassette, or reels of 1″ video tape. Here again, time coding if appropriate can save time in the bay. Copying library music to tape may not be required unless a razor blade edit is necessary. Transfer of a cue directly from a record album to a multitrack ATR is explained in the chapter on techniques.

There are two benefits in copying sound effects from record to tape. First is accessibility. Having all the effects recorded sequentially on one tape saves time pulling records. Second, it is faster and easier to position synchronized effects coming from tape.

Some sound effects may not be found in libraries; the alternative is to manufacture effects. This can be a very creative part of the preparation for sweetening. Techniques for creating effects will be discussed in later chapters. In gathering and preparing materials, the goal once again is to have all the effects organized and accessible.

If your project calls for original music, the producer plays a special role in the interface between the client, composer, and music producer in preparing the music tracks before the actual sweetening takes place. Chapter 9 discusses the producer's tasks in producing original music. At the end of that process, the producer will be holding an audio tape in the proper format for the sweetening bay, probably time coded, ready to lay over to the multitrack ATR.

When you are finished gathering your materials, you will have separate reels for music, SFX, narration, background presence fill, etc., each having the specific cues in the order they will be used. In most cases these will be on 1/4″ tape, except for what is already on video tape or cassette. Under certain conditions, audio cassettes may be used. High-quality audio cassettes are perfectly acceptable for "wild" sounds, presence, and background sounds, and are also very good for sound effects because of their fast start time.

A note about 1/4″ editing, an inevitable part of the preparation process is appropriate here: If you sweeten yourself, as opposed to having it done for you at a sweetening house, then you must master the skill of editing on 1/4″ audio tape. In the era of electronic editing, it may seem a bit anachronistic to step back to the days of razor blades; however, editing 1/4″ or 1/2″ audio tape with a razor blade is most efficient once the technique is mastered and it is a simple technique to master with only a little practice. There are a variety of situations that may necessitate editing audio tape, including making a music cue fit a certain timing sequence and editing narration and other "wild" or non-sync dialog or interview tracks.

Gathering and preparing source materials will often be the most time-consuming phase of sweetening. But to repeat, a thorough job of preparation will save hours in the editing room or the sweetening bay.

LAYDOWN

Enter the sweetening bay, arms loaded with reels of audio tape, library music records, and video cassettes, spotting sheets, source notes, and a video edited master plus its window dub. The room is hot. A multitrack ATR is loaded with a reel of audio tape, waiting to be filled with the audio elements of your program. Where to start? The laydown.

The *laydown* is the process of transferring an edited audio track from the edited master video tape to the multitrack ATR. One or perhaps two audio tracks were edited in the video edit. Depending on equipment and strategy, this is either a scratch track for reference or a finished, clean track. This track usually will be on-camera dialog and natural sounds from video tape sources, or narration and music required for timing video edits (for example, a visual montage edited to music). If you have taken care during the video editing process to make "clean" audio edits, then this track will be used as one of the elements during the final mix. Even if you haven't taken such care, or intend that the audio track from the EM be used only as a scratch track, you must still lay it down to the multitrack ATR for use as a reference during the track-building step.

If you have on-lined either 3/4″ to 1″ interformat, or 1″ to 1″ and have made use of both audio channels on the 1″ EM (such as for production audio on one channel and music or narration on the other), then you will want to lay down both of these tracks on the multitrack ATR. By recording on two tracks of the 1″ edited master, you will save yourself much time in assembling or otherwise building audio tracks that are easier to build during on-line editing.

Laydown is the place where audio and video are first divorced and the requirement for synchronization arises (Fig. 2-5). With the audio and video recorded on separate media, it becomes necessary to run two tape decks synchronously to see and hear the full program during sweetening and later to transfer the final audio back to the edited master video tape. Thorough discussion of the hows and whys of synchronization will follow in later chapters, but accept here the following fact: Time code is the link between the audio

Fig. 2-5. The laydown, or placing the edited audio track from the edited master video tape (EM) is the first step that uses the equipment. It requires time code on the multitrack tape reel, as well as having both the multitrack ATR and the VTR under the control of a synchronizer or edit controller such as the CMX Edge pictured here. In this photo, Fred Hull is setting up an event to transfer the audio from the record VTR (a Sony 5850) to the TASCAM 58 8-track ATR directly above it.

and video tapes that enables synchronization; therefore, the proper relationship of audio tracks and time code must be established in the laydown.

Two methods for laydown exists. The audio tape may be precoded and the edited audio track is transferred with the two machines, VTR and ATR, running in sync under control of a synchronizer or edit controller. Alternately, the laydown may be a free-running recording from VTR to ATR, with time code from the VTR recorded to one track of the ATR in parallel with the audio program track(s). Recording simultaneously guarantees the relationship between code and program audio.

A technical note: Purists would say that it is bad practice to dub time code because generational degradation of the signal can render it unreadable. The authors' experience using hi-fi audio equipment, U-matic and 1″ VTRs, and modern time code readers is that dubbing time code *once* is fully reliable. Though it is not recommended, circumstances have required dubbing code to third-generation; even this has proven acceptable.

If the time code is recorded from the EM to the ATR, the two will, of course, be numerically identical. If the audio tape is precoded, it can be synchronized to the EM even though its time code may not be numerically equal. Nonidentical time code will work throughout the sweetening, but having identical time code will prove to be much easier to deal with, both in the thinking processes and in the machine control. If the option is available, request identical time code on the multitrack audio tape and the edited master.

BUILDING TRACKS

The track-building process, as the term implies, consists of recording each of the elements that together make up the complete soundtrack onto the multitrack ATR. The plan or script for this process is the *spotting sheet*. The raw materials are all the music cues, sound effects, presence loops, etc., collected in the gathering stage. The goal is to record each of these audio elements onto various tracks of the ATR at the proper time in the program, i.e., corresponding to the proper visual element, so that all of those tracks can be mixed together to produce the complete soundtrack. While recording the cues and effects in their synchronized positions is half the objective, equally important is making the recording sound good.

So there are really two facets to this task. One is machine control, similar to editing—manipulating the ATRs, VTRs, phonographs, etc. to allow the properly synchronized recording. The

18

other is audio engineering—routing signals, setting levels and equalization, controlling signal processing, and adding special effects. As such, this process is often most efficient with two people, the control person and the audio person; in more "official" terminology, they are the (sweetening) editor and the audio engineer.

A secondary objective in this process is to build the tracks so that the mix is easy. The more time spent in making the tracks right in terms of accurate in- and out-points, relative levels and contours, and quality of sound, the easier the mix will be. Usually the effort invested in building the track for easy mix is far less than the extra effort required to conform that track during the mix.

The preceding steps of the audio sweetening process, spotting and gathering materials, have been identical to those of film; it is in the track-building step that the ease of computer intelligence replaces the mechanical methods of film. The synchronizer or edit controller (these will be fully explained in Chapter 5) interlocks the picture VTR and the audio machine by reading each machine's time code and locking them together. The synchronizer also has the ability to lock or "slave" several additional machines to the time code, as well as start and stop the other machines and actuate the record function on the multitrack recorder. The record function also can be actuated manually.

If all the source machines were linked to the control device, this process would be very similar to editing audio in a video edit. In practice, rarely are all the machines under time code control, especially in the small-scale sweetening environment. Manual control must be intermixed with synchronized control. Learning to deal with a variety of machines and how to best use each to accomplish the building of synchronized and semisynchronized tracks is a challenging prospect.

Making the remaining track assignments (if this has not been done during the spotting session) is the first step in track building (Fig. 2-6). This generally means arbitrarily deciding for example, that SFX reel one will be placed on track 3, SFX reel two on track 4, music on track 5, narration on the track 6, fill or background presence material on track 7, etc. In some circumstances this will be not quite arbitrary. Working with many tightly packed sources or limited tracks can be like solving a jigsaw puzzle, trying to find open spaces for all the cues and effects. Some tracks have already been used for code and laydown and one or two tracks may be reserved for the mix. Technical considerations, such as a guard band for the time code track or the potential for feedback in the mix, also affect the assignment of tracks. These technical considerations

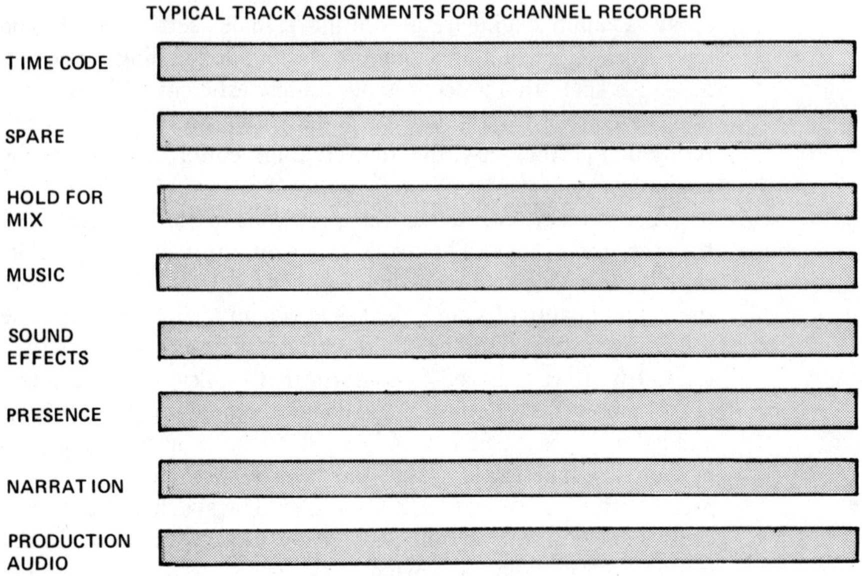

TYPICAL TRACK ASSIGNMENTS FOR 8 CHANNEL RECORDER

TIME CODE	
SPARE	
HOLD FOR MIX	
MUSIC	
SOUND EFFECTS	
PRESENCE	
NARRATION	
PRODUCTION AUDIO	

Fig. 2-6. Track relationships on an 8-track ATR used for audio sweetening.

will be discussed later.

With tracks assigned, recording begins. Start at the beginning of the program and lay in all elements chronologically, or work first on all music or all effects; the procedure will vary from person to person and program to program. Each music cue, sound effect, narration piece, and bit of fill material is added, one by one, to its predefined channel, at its predefined time code address on the multitrack ATR.

It will save you a lot of time during the final mix if you premix the elements during the track-building process. If you know when a cue or effect must fade up or out, or know what its volume level needs to be vis-a-vis other material, then make such adjustments (including EQ) when you lay an element down on the multitrack. This way, most of the tough work will be done before the final mix, making the mix itself a less hectic event.

If you need to split actors' dialog from a single track on the edited master to separate tracks on the ATR, it should be done at this point. That dialog may be retrieved from the original field masters or from the EM. It might be necessary to equalize the tracks from the original field masters to match what was recorded on the multitrack during the laydown.

Throughout track building, check carefully that each item is laid down on the multitrack machine in the correct position by watching the picture in sync with the ATR. Carefully listen to make sure you are satisfied with the audio quality. Building the tracks right at this time will save countless headaches later.

MIXING THE TRACKS

Mixing is the stage of the process where all of the discrete audio elements, now strewn across many tracks of the ATR, are combined into a unified soundtrack. Anyone in the production business already knows what audio mixing is, has probably tried it some time, and needs little explanation of the concept. For anyone else, mixing is an electronic summation of several audio signals, creating a new signal representing the composite sound one would hear if all the individual sources were played simultaneously. In the mixing process, the relative volume of each source is regulated to mold the overall character of the final track. Often the audio signals are electronically processed during the mix to subtly alter their tonal quality—or even to radically affect the sound. The controlled summation of all the tracks and all the effects is the final program audio, so this is the time to make it sound the way you have imagined it.

The first technical lesson in mixing is how to mix; that is, what equipment is used, what sounds go from where to where, and how all the ingredients are controlled. With that knowledge and a concept of the desired result, you can begin mixing a soundtrack. The second technical lesson in mixing is how to tailor that mix as you conceived it for the distribution medium. There are, of course, thousands of artistic lessons of mixing learned only through hours of listening and mixing and listening and mixing.

For the mixing operation, each of the ATR channels with elements of the soundtrack is connected to an input of the mixing console. Through the console the signals are routed and mixed into one or more outputs. The outputs are connected to the recording inputs of either the same ATR, another ATR, or a VTR. As the ATR plays, the operator manipulates the levels, the equalization, and the special effects processing to color the mix precisely. As he does this, the mixed track or tracks are recorded. The available sweetening equipment and individual project circumstances will dictate where the mix track or tracks are recorded.

Mixing can be an audio-only process, but watching the picture simultaneously is helpful in anticipating upcoming cues and effects and in exercising the aesthetic controls. Mixing to picture is a simple matter of synchronizing the program VTR to the audio deck(s) with a synchronizer or edit controller.

For the typical television program, broadcast or industrial, all the audio is mixed into a single soundtrack for monaural television sets. Some programs, however, require mixing to two tracks and others to three tracks. Stereo audio obviously is a two-track mix. When a program will be distributed in several countries, a two-track mix allows separating the dialog and/or narration from the music and sound effects. Translations of the "verbal" track may be integrated without a remix of the other audio elements. This principle of separating mix tracks applies other times when some portion of the soundtrack, such as theme music may change. Following the "three-stripe" convention of the film industry, three independent tracks are mixed—dialog, music, and effects. These three are then mixed into the final monaural soundtrack.

The choice of single- or multiple-track mixes may affect the execution process. Recording a two- or three-track mix back to the principal ATR is often impossible because the tracks are not available; thus, a second multitrack ATR must be used to record the mix. For a stereo audio mix, the two tracks must be mixed simultaneously, whereas other dual-track audio may be mixed one at a time.

In some cases the mix will be recorded back to an open track on the same ATR, in which case the mix is inevitably synchronized to the program time code. Another option is to record the mixed track(s) onto another ATR, a possibility if tracks are not vacant on the source ATR. A third possibility would be to record the mix directly to the edited master video tape. This is a combination of the mix and the yet-to-be-discussed layback process. If the mix is not recorded back to the source ATR, the record deck must be synchronized with time code to the source deck to guarantee that the program audio is or later can be synchronized with the program picture, and that the mix can be resumed after stopping in the middle of the program. If the mix can be accomplished in one pass, as in perhaps a very short program or a TV spot, it could be recorded to another ATR without interlock. The time code from the source ATR would be recorded simultaneously for use in the layback, but beware of time code degeneration. Test the process before relying on it.

Realistically, the mix will be a trial-and-error, repetitive process. Rolling from the top of the show, audio sources patched and ready, picture VTR interlocked, recording tracks (or deck) enabled, the mix begins. From this point, this is a live performance of a complicated process; like any performance, it's not likely that it will be perfect from beginning to end in one pass. When something is recognized as less than optimal, stop. Modern ATRs can be set into record mode while playing, much like an insert edit on a editing video tape deck. To continue the mix, rewind the tape to a good section, start the deck(s) in play mode, and at some point "punch in" to record mode. The whole track is generally made in many overlapping sections. Similarly, the ATR allows "Punch out" on the fly to stop recording. Thus it is possible to remix a section and leave the following track intact. Audio characteristics of the punch-in and punch-out points will be discussed in Chapter 6.

To simplify a very complicated mix job or to incorporate more sources than track capacity would otherwise allow, it is often helpful to mix subtracks (Fig 2-7). The term for this is *predubbing* or *sub-mixing*, and it is a form of the recording industry technique of "ping-ponging." If you are using an 8-track ATR and have a very complicated show, this process might be necessary. You simply mix several tracks (all the sound effects tracks, for example) into one track, and then use that one track as the source when you run the final mix. Clearly this will simplify intricate sections. And, if you run out of available tracks, erase the original effects tracks and keep only the composite effects track.

An example of this situation would be if you have a program that has a very complicated sound effects sequence—the industrial-scale *Star Wars*, if you will. Due to the complexity of the tracks, comprised of a number of discrete elements such as laser-gun shots,

Fig. 2-7. Mixing the tracks is one of the most critical steps in the sweetening process. Depending on the length and complexity of the program, mixing can take hours, days, or weeks to complete.

23

ricochets, grunts and groans from talent, background presence, etc., all requiring delicate mixing, you may have filled up many of the available source tracks on the multitrack, leaving no room for music and narration. Consequently, you must first premix the elaborate effects sequence down to one track. Depending on the actual complexity of the effects sequence, this may require several attempts, stopping, going back, punching back into record and making the fixes necessary for a perfect mix. Once you are satisfied with the premix then you may erase the primary source tracks, making room for other elements such as music and narration, before making the final mix of the show.

Evaluating the mix is a key issue in the sweetening game. The standards of quality applied to the mix must be derived from the intended delivery media and devices. When you dub or mix for film, typically you must assume that the show will ultimately be projected in a large theater with a good sound system; the audio quality will be recognized. If you have mastered in video tape and know that the product will end up in small-format distribution, played back on consumer television sets, you can get away with a lot more. Let's face it, 3/4" or 1/2" does not demand super broadcast or movie theater quality. A hole, glitch, or EQ differential may be undetectable when played through a TV speaker, even if it's a whopping 6 × 9 incher. No producer enjoys cutting corners or lowering standards, but if you spend precious sweetening time (at $100 or $200 per hour) fixing things that no viewer will ever notice, you may be risking the budget unnecessarily.

Typically, studio quality speakers are used in a sweetening bay, during the mixing process, giving the optimum sound. However, since television shows seldom are played through such fine monitors, it is good practice to listen also through a set of smaller speakers, more representative of television speakers. After hearing something questionable during the mixing process, you can easily stop and play it back through the TV speaker to determine whether it will be detectable in the field. If you can hear the imperfection through the TV speaker, then go back and fix it; if not, you may consider leaving it and continuing the mix.

When you reach the end and have mixed the entire show, take a break; you'll deserve it. Then go back to the beginning of the show for a fresh look and play it back, review it, and make fixes. It is rare that you will not find a couple of things that require re-equalizing or refining.

You can continue to mix, remix, and fix things for an entire career—on one program. The question you must ask yourself is, "Am I making it *better* or just *different?*" You have to know when

Fig. 2-8. Taking the opportunity for a fresh look and listen will always yield changes that can be made. The question to ask is whether the change will make the program better or just different.

to walk away from a mixing session, much like knowing when to walk away from an edit, and say, "That's as good as I can make it," or "That's as good as it needs to be," due to budget or time constraints (Fig. 2-8).

LAYBACK

The layback is the final step in the sweetening process—transferring the final mixed soundtrack back to the edited master video tape. Naturally the audio must be returned to the EM in sync with the picture; hence the layback is controlled by the synchronizer. In typical Hollywood sweetening, this is most often performed at the sweetening house, recording from 24-track ATR to 1″ VTR. Alternatively, a sweetening house without a 1″ VTR might send the mix out on a time-coded 1/2″ audio tape to be laid back to 1″ video in the video edit house under control of the video edit controller. Possibly the layback is not necessary at all if the track was mixed directly to the EM.

In the simplest case, the layback is a direct, one-channel recording from the ATR to the VTR. A stereo program requires a two-channel layback. If a split mix was prepared on the ATR, there is a choice here to lay back the two tracks separately to two chan-

25

Fig. 2-9. The layback is an automated step in the sweetening process. It requires setting up through the edit controller or synchronizer controller an event which records the mixed audio track from the multitrack ATR to the edited master (EM) video tape. It is the final step in the sweetening process.

Fig. 2-10. The Sony/MCI layback machine facilitates the layback process to 1″ video tape without tying up an expensive 1″ VTR (courtesy Sony Corporation).

nels of the VTR, or to mix the two in layback. If the "three-stripe" method is used, then the three tracks must be mixed in the layback (Figs. 2-9 and 2-10).

As stated earlier, the preceding steps of the process may not be executed exactly in the order presented. Individual methods will necessarily be customized to available facilities and project requirements. Whatever the operating order to this point, the layback finishes the sweetening process and, with luck, that puts the program in the can.

Chapter 3

Recording Production Audio

re • cord • ing \ ri- ′ kȯrd-iŋ \ *n* the registering of
sound, as on a video or audio tape, with reference to the
relative quality of reproduction afforded

This chapter deals with some basic audio hardware and basic audio
techniques. This is intended only as an overview of audio recording as it pertains to video and video sweetening. There are
many volumes in print concerning audio recording in general, and
you are encouraged to consult some other books for a more detailed
discussion of this topic. On audio recording in general, you are re-
ferred to Robert E. Runstein's *Modern Recording Techniques*,
published 1974 by Howard W. Sams & Co. For more information
on microphones, refer to *Microphones: Design and Application*, by
Lou Burroughs, Sagamore Publishing Company, Inc., 1974.

Although the aspects of audio recording discussed in this
chapter are not technically part of the sweetening process, we feel
that a good basic understanding of audio recording will always help
in the sweetening process. First, you may be able to record more
trouble-free tracks in the field or audio studio; second, understanding some basic audio recording principle will make it easier
and quicker to correct or minimize problems that may exist in the
sweetening process. The goal of this chapter is to assist you in getting better audio tracks before the sweetening process actually

begins, in order to make the sweetening process easier. Also, please note that the sweetening process can not always fix every audio problem, only sweeten. This means that the sweetening process more often that not is one of making educated compromises to make the audio track more pleasing than it would be without the sweetening. The point is that the better the audio tracks are before sweetening commences, the better they will be when sweetening is completed.

BASIC AUDIO HARDWARE

Recording good audio requires mastering some basic concepts and specifics regarding audio hardware and devices. This section discusses balanced lines, microphones, cables, audio and video tape decks and mixers. If the reader is already comfortable with this hardware, you may wish to move ahead to "Basic Audio Recording Techniques."

Balanced and Unbalanced Lines

Without wading through a detailed technical discussion, you should be aware that *balanced* and *unbalanced lines* exist in the audio realm. The coexistence of these different lines can be a source of problems and frustration, even for the experienced audio professional. The video person needs to recognize the potential for audio problems in this area.

In audio, a line is the wire or cable that carries a signal from one place to another. This may be from a microphone to a mixer to a tape deck, from a tape deck to another tape deck, or any place else one wishes a audio signal to be carried. The line can be balanced or unbalanced. If the line is *balanced* the cable carrying the signal needs three wires. Two of the wires carry the signal (high and low) and one, which is also the outside shield, carries the audio ground. The *unbalanced line* has only two wires. One carries the signal and one, the shield, carries the audio ground. Connectors on the wire usually have three or more connection points for a balanced line and two connection points for an unbalanced line. Many problems arise from using connectors with three or more connection points, such as a standard XLR microphone connector used to connect an unbalanced line. There are no standard methods for doing this, but it seems as if there is always a need to do it. Some equipment manufacturers have both balanced and unbalanced connections for inputs and outputs. Others have one or the other. To complicate matters further, some manufacturers call pin 2 of an XLR connector high in a balanced line, while some call pin 3 high.

The only thing commonly agreed on is that pin one is always ground. Some equipment will work with either pin 2 or 3 high, while others will not.

Balanced line inputs and outputs are found on most professional audio equipment. Balanced lines are usually better than unbalanced lines for several reasons. They can be as long as you need with no appreciable loss in frequency response or signal level. As a rule, unbalanced lines should not be more than 20 feet long, if possible. Balanced lines do a much better job of eliminating unwanted interference such as fluorescent light buzz, radio stations, electric motor noise, etc. Why doesn't all equipment incorporate balanced lines? Because, in general, it is more expensive to build equipment that way. Some of the more recent professional equipment uses unbalanced lines, but into a low-impedance load. (Unbalanced lines usually go into a high-impedance load.) Unbalanced lines into a low impedance load can be run for long distances; however, the issue of which XLR pin is hot becomes extremely important, since one way you would have signal and the other way you would have no signal at all. In order to interconnect audio equipment properly, it is necessary to be aware of line types and input/output impedance characteristics. The equipment manuals and your audio dealer or engineer will be the best source for this information and the key to proper interconnection.

Microphone Types

Microphones, along with cables, are probably the most overlooked items to the video person having to record audio. Understanding the type, pattern, and quality of the microphone can greatly benefit anyone recording an audio track.

There are four basic types of microphones in common use today. They are dynamic, condenser, Pressure Zone Microphone (PZM) and ribbon. Outside of the audio recording studio, the *ribbon microphone* is rarely used because of its fragility, and will not be discussed here. The dynamic and condenser microphones are widely used, and the PZM is finding a variety of uses, especially in more unusual circumstances.

The *dynamic microphone* is the most common microphone in use today. It is very rugged and usually a good choice for field recording, especially for hand-held use. It requires no external power source; there are no power supplies or dead batteries to worry about. It is less sensitive to wind and hand-held noises than the condenser microphone. This can be a plus or a minus, depending on the situation. Where wind is a problem, a dynamic microphone with a wind screen is by far your best choice. However, if increased sensitivity is desired, the condenser or PZM may be a better choice. One other drawback to dynamic microphones in general is a decreased sensitivity to higher audio frequencies above 8000 Hz compared to condenser and PZM microphones. Depending on the application and situation, this may or may not be a problem in a video shoot. If audio is being recorded to a 1″ video or reel-to-reel audio deck, a difference may be noticed. If audio is being recorded to 3/4″ or 1/2″ video, the difference would not be noticed when played back from the tape. All in all, every video shoot where usable audio is needed, should have one or more dynamic microphones available.

As mentioned above, condenser microphones are more sensitive and usually have a flatter frequency response than dynamic microphones. However, these benefits do not come without some trade-offs. Condenser microphones have a preamplifier built into the microphone; this produces a higher microphone output, but requires power for the microphone to work at all. Most modern condenser microphones get their power from a battery or batteries in the microphone or from a *phantom power* source.

In solid-state condenser microphones, this power source is always direct current. Sometimes battery-powered microphones, especially lavaliers, have a separate box or container to house the batteries. Phantom-powered microphones get their direct current power from the microphone input of the mixing desk. The microphone input puts a direct current voltage on the high and low pins of a balanced line microphone. The microphone puts an alternating current signal on the balanced line, back to the microphone input. Then the input filters out the direct current voltage, and only the signal from the microphone remains. Phantom power can work only with balanced line microphones.

Obviously, when preparing for a shoot you must know what types of microphones you have and what type you need. Fresh, new batteries should always be on the pack-out list for any shoot using battery-powered condenser microphones. Batteries in some condenser microphones may last for only an hour, while others may last for days. However, it is never wise to risk being caught with your batteries down.

The only drawback to condenser microphones, apart from needing power, is that some of them do not work well in wind. However, many of the better condensers do quite well with a wind screen. Since they are quite sensitive, they usually do a better job of picking up the sound you need when you must keep the microphone out of the picture. It is also a good idea, and many times a must, to have one or more condenser microphones on any shoot requiring usable audio.

Pressure Zone Microphones (the term is a trademark of Crown International) are in some ways a subset of condenser microphones. All PZMs need power to operate, just as condenser microphones do, but the operating principle differs. Instead of letting the air waves vibrate a membrane (as in condenser, dynamic, or ribbon microphones), the PZM's output varies with the changing pressure in the "zone" between the element and a fixed plate. The main difference between condenser and PZM-type microphones, however, is in the pickup pattern, which will be discussed later.

Although Crown developed the concept and patented it, there are other manufacturers who also make PZM-type microphones. Because of Crown's patent, these mics differ in appearance from the Crown product, but they can be used in exactly the same way. For example, the fixed plate is built as part of the Crown PZM, while other manufacturers' elements need to be mounted on a separate plate. (Crown recommends that their own PZM be mounted on a larger plate, depending on the situation and desired use.)

Microphone Patterns

The *pattern* of a microphone means its pickup pattern, i.e., the sensitivity of the microphone to the position of the sound source. The common pickup patterns are omnidirectional, cardioid, supercardioid or shotgun, bidirectional, and hemispherical. In understanding microphones, you need to be careful not to confuse the type and the pattern of the microphone. They are independent.

These pickup patterns are illustrated in Fig. 3-1. The patterns are just a visual way of showing a microphone's sensitivity to direction. Omnidirectional microphones are equally sensitive to sound coming from all directions. In other words, there is really no front or back to the microphone. The cardioid pattern picks up from the front much more strongly than from any other direction. The supercardioid or shotgun is similar to the cardioid but still more directional, and does not pick up as much from the sides. The bidirectional pattern picks up from the front and back equally, while strongly rejecting the sides. The hemispherical pattern picks up from all directions in front of the microphone equally well while picking up almost no sound from all directions behind the microphone. This particular pattern is unique to the PZM-type microphones.

PZM-type microphones definitely are not meant to be handheld, and really would be of no use in that manner. However, what they do well is hard to do better with any other pickup pattern. For example, one microphone in the middle of a conference table

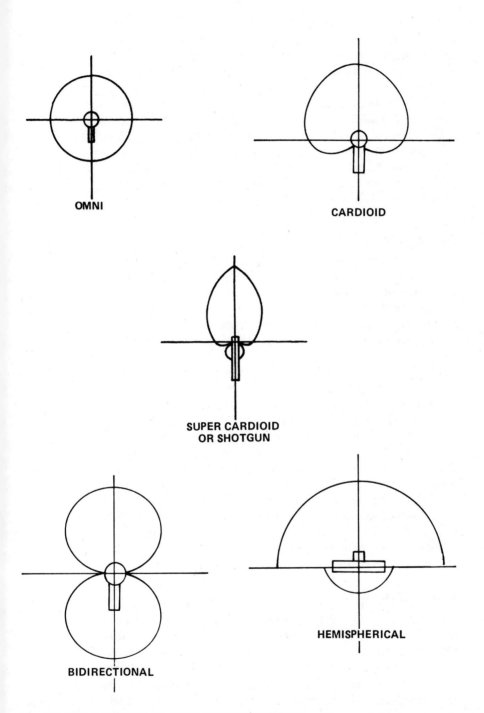

OMNI

CARDIOID

SUPER CARDIOID
OR SHOTGUN

BIDIRECTIONAL

HEMISPHERICAL

Fig. 3-1. Pickup pattern of five common microphone types.

will pick up everyone around the table equally. They are also great for ambient sounds on location or in the field. One (or two in stereo) can work very well for picking up large groups of people, whether they are talking, singing, or playing in a symphony orchestra. Sound reinforcement people often mic a grand piano by taping a PZM to the underside of the lid. Remember, both the advantage and disadvantage of this type of microphone is that it does not differentiate direction from the front, and does not pick up from the back. If the sound source moves sideways in front of the microphone, the microphone will not be able to tell the difference as long as it stays in the front hemisphere. Of course, moving closer or farther away will affect the volume, but moving sideways will not.

Lavalier Microphones

Everyone who works in the video field has to deal with lavalier microphones. Some producers and sound people swear by them, while the rest swear at them. Lavalier microphones, which can be dynamic or condenser, usually have an omnidirectional pattern, although some are cardioid. These microphones do present some unique problems of their own, usually having to do with clothing noise, or keeping talent from tripping on the cord. Care must be taken in placing the microphone to minimize clothing noise. Usually a little experimenting along with some common sense will help.

Try to put the microphone where it cannot rub against the clothes at all; if you try to hide the microphone from the camera, the chance of clothing noise increases greatly. Placing the mic under neckties or blouses can work well, but care must be taken so that the audio does not sound covered, as if the talent were talking through a blanket. This means that you have to place the microphone as close to the throat as possible. Hiding the cable from the camera is sometimes a problem, but can usually be done by running the cable through the talent's clothes to the floor. If the talent is walking or moving around while on camera, you probably will need someone to pull or otherwise guide the cable.

Wireless Microphones

There are a few different varieties of wireless microphones, most intended for lavalier or hand-held use, varying in cost from $300 to more than $2000. Most of the less expensive models (under $700) can be used only in tightly controlled recording situations; they are capable of good results, but equally often you may find them unusable. The quality of a particular wireless mic is usually apparent on first use; you are wise to buy quality if you expect to use one in a variety of situations.

Another note about wireless microphones: Most of them have some compression built into the transmitter to improve the signal to noise ratio. The amount of compression often will be affected by the level control on the transmitter. When the microphone over-compresses, the sound can be quite annoying and unusable. If this is a problem, you need to turn down the volume on the transmitter and turn up the volume at the receiver or mixer. These microphones have to have their gain structured properly in order to realize their best performance. If you are not familiar with your wireless microphone, you need to try it out and work with it. Try different volume settings and see what works the best for a few different settings. This will be time well spent and will avoid many embarrassing and frustrating situations in the long run.

Cables

All of us in the video or audio business have to deal with cables, usually lots of cables. Not only are you connecting and disconnecting them, you're replacing them, finding them, losing them, fixing them, and wishing you had brought along more of them as well as more adapters. Cables, without any moving parts, seem to be the least likely candidate for things to go wrong. Why is it then, that somewhere around 90 percent of all audio problems have something to do with cables?

If we were to treat out 95-cent cables with the same respect as our $15,000 camera, we would have fewer problems with them. Cabling for a shoot needs to be planned with the same importance as the rest of the equipment. Make sure you have the right cables and spares. Make sure you have enough length of each type of cable. Also, make sure you have some adapters and a variety of cable ends to take care of the situations that you never thought you would encounter. It is never a good idea to use more adapters than you need, but they definitely are nice to have around. The probability of a cable problem increases as the mathematical square of the number of cable connections. It is always best to have the right cable, with the right ends and in the right length, for every cable connection. Although in real life this never happens, it is still a worthwhile goal for which to strive.

All of your cables should always be kept clean. They should always be neatly coiled, without sharp bends, and tied or taped together. It is best to coil them the same way every time, following their natural twist. They will coil and uncoil much easier, save countless hours of untangling, and last longer as well. There is a very great quality difference among cables and cable manufacturers.

As with most things, the better cables cost more money. Also, the better quality cables will save more money in the long run, and decrease the number of your headaches. But, they have to be cared for, just as much as any other equipment you use.

Audio Tape Decks

Audio recorded for video use is usually done on a reel-to-reel audio tape deck, or directly to video tape. Video tape is the easiest and least hassle, but yields the lower audio quality of the two. Reel-to-reel gives you very high quality audio. In film or video, this is usually done with a Nagra tape deck, or some other deck that can run in sync with video tape during postproduction. It usually takes another person or operator on the shoot but when done properly, the extra effort gives extremely high-quality audio tracks. When recording audio in the field or studio with reel-to-reel or video recorders, always make sure the deck is clean. The best policy is to clean it after each use, and it does not hurt to clean it before each use. This is a very important and often overlooked item. Clean *everything* in the tape path, i.e., tape guides, heads and drums, pinch rollers, capstan, etc. And always test your deck before the shoot and *listen* to the tape; don't be satisfied just to see that the needles on the meters move.

Make sure you have some good-quality headphones or speakers to really "hear" what is on the tape. Especially if you are recording on video tape, you'll often need to augment the deck's headphone system with another amplifier. Most headphone amplifiers built into video decks do not let you listen at a high enough volume to detect potential problems. In addition, the better quality headphones usually are less efficient, needing more power to drive them—almost always more than is available in video decks.

This may seem like a small item, but I have been able to save much valuable time on a shoot by listening carefully while shooting is going on. However, this can only be done if the headphones are loud enough to hear over the room noise, or over the sound you are actually recording. In this way, you can hear mistakes or problems when they happen, saving time in unnecessary playbacks. The headphones can be driven with a small, low-cost, home stereo amplifier. It is well worth the effort for good-sounding audio tracks.

If you are rerecording over previously recorded tape, whether reel-to-reel audio or video, it is always a good idea to degauss (erase) the tape before the shoot. It saves time, confusion, and sometimes embarrassment during playback and/or postproduction. A variety of "bulk erasers" is available, usually for less than $50.

Audio Mixers

Audio mixers or consoles are used to combine or mix together different inputs, such as four microphones to be recorded onto mono video tape, or any other combination of inputs from microphones, tape decks, records, etc., to a monophonic or stereo output. There are many types, sizes, and qualities of mixing consoles currently available. One of the smaller varieties usually is all that is needed for a video shoot.

On location, you have the fewest problems when you keep everything as simple as possible. Do not rent a 24-channel mixer to mix two microphones to a mono videotape. Shure, Sony and other manufacturers make battery-powered mixers that can be very useful for outside or remote locations. Although there are literally hundreds of different features available on mixing consoles, all you need for location recording is to be able to individually control the levels of each microphone, and perhaps some equalization on each channel. This is all that is necessary unless it is a large or complicated shoot, or if live music is being recorded. In that case, you first need to hire a good sound person to tell you what equipment you need and proceed from there.

BASIC AUDIO RECORDING

This section presents some basic audio recording principles and techniques specifically relating to audio for video. First we will look at some basic techniques and pointers. Then we will look at the more specific areas of recording.

Basic Techinques

Setup and Miking. A little advance planning is always beneficial to an efficient shoot. Plan out the microphones, cables and cable lengths, mixer, outboard equipment, recording tape deck, and recording tape. When planning your setup, consider the different possibilities and situations that may occur during the shoot. If you are not sure about how to mic the talent (whether to use a shotgun on a boom or a lavalier,) for example set up for both ways. Always try to allow for extra microphone cable length. Then you can easily try them both; no one will feel any extra pressure, and time will not be wasted. The more professionally you approach the shoot, the more professionally the rest of the crew and talent will approach the shoot.

Listen. Always listen carefully. Listen to the microphones and other inputs during setup and rehearsal. If you listen carefully, and with some experience, you will be able to tell what problems may exist and correct them before anyone else notices. The types of noises, distortion, pops, and clicks you hear will usually lead you to the problem much faster if you listen well and use a little common sense. Also, always listen to the tape before you call it a "wrap" at any one location. If you use headphones, make sure you are able to listen loud enough to hear what is really there. You may need to use the auxiliary amplifier discussed earlier.

Level Setting. In order to obtain optimum audio quality in any audio recording, you need to have the audio levels as high as possible without distortion. This keeps the level of the recorded signal at its maximum above the inherent tape hiss (the "noise floor") present in any analog recording medium. If the levels are too high, however, distortion will result from saturation, i.e., trying to make the recording tape hold more level than is possible. This distortion will make that portion of the audio track unusable. It is safer to have your levels a little too low than a little too high. Assuming you have properly calibrated meters, it usually is best to set the overall recording level so that the needle peaks at zero VU.

A note is in order here regarding setting level for on-camera talent: The real take almost always will have hotter signal levels than during the rehearsal or setup. There is something about human nature that gets people more excited and intense when they know the performance is for real, even with professionals. Don't simply set your levels and walk away. It is also a good idea to be a little on the conservative side, so that you do not have to ruin an otherwise good take or spend valuable time "riding gain" on the mixer if the levels happen to get louder than you expected. If the recording deck you are using has built in limiting or compression, you should always set your levels with these features switched out or off.

Compressing and Limiting. *Compressing* an audio signal is an electronic way of riding the volume control, thus reducing the *dynamic range* of the signal, i.e., the difference between the loudest and softest parts. Compression makes the soft parts louder and the loud parts softer, much faster than you could ever do by hand. It also is done uniformly, at a ratio called the *compression ratio*. For most normal applications this ratio would range from 2:1 to 5:1. When this ratio is much higher, over 10:1, it is called *limiting*. While compression works on all of the audio signal, i.e., the louds and the softs, limiting generally just works on the louds above a threshold. In some equipment, including most VCRs with built-in limiting, this threshold is preset. In other equipment, such as outboard compressor/limiters, the threshold is variable.

Compressing and limiting are useful to help control the dynamic range, so that recording levels can be high enough to increase the signal-to-noise ratio, but to keep the short, louder parts of the audio from overloading the audio tape. Compressors and limiters can be useful in postproduction as well, but their use there is beyond the scope of this discussion. On a shoot, it is best to use compression or limiting as little as possible. However, this would normally mean having an audio person monitor the recording levels at all times. If you don't have such a person on the crew, the best compromise is to set your levels on the conservative side, that is, peaking at -5dB to -3dB, and use a built-in limiter if you have one. This is especially true if you are recording audio to video tape. Some of the older VCRs had compressors built in; most of the more recent varieties have switchable limiters, if anything at all. Portable reel-to-reel decks such as Nagras also have a switchable limiter built in, but studio reel-to-reel audio decks rarely have any built-in signal processing.

Equalization. *Equalization* (EQ) is the adding or taking away of frequencies to or from an audio signal. This can be as simple as the tone control on your car radio, or it could be a complicated piece of outboard equipment such as a parametric equalizer. For a video shoot equalization normally would be done at the mixing board, most of which have some type of equalization for each input of the board. It may be two-band (treble and bass), or it may be four- or five-band. This gives you more control over the sounds, voices, or music you are recording. You can add high frequencies or treble to brighten a voice and make it more understandable. Or you may wish to take out some of the air conditioner noise in the background by taking out some of the lower frequencies or bass.

Used sensibly, equalization can make postproduction much easier, or maybe even save a poor audio track. Equalization should only be used to make a sound more like what you want, or to help get rid of some of the sounds you do not want, such as background noise. If you are in doubt whether to EQ something, it is probably best not to. Make any final decisions in postproduction. However, if you know what you want and you have the time to try it out with EQ, then it can be very helpful.

Equalization is one of the most valuable audio tools you have, both in original recording and postproduction, but it is something that takes a little practice to use effectively. However, some time spent experimenting with EQ will be well worth it.

Wind and Background Sounds. On location, wind and background noise can present many problems. Learn to use your microphones to your advantage. For example, if wind is a problem while recording live sounds, use a cardioid or shotgun-pattern microphone, with a wind screen, with the back of the microphone into the wind. This puts the least sensitive side of the microphone where the wind is the strongest. Wind can sometimes be minimized with equalization. However, if there is distortion from the microphone because of wind, equalization or bringing the level down will not get rid of it, though you can make it less noticeable. In this case the distortion would be coming from the microphone, and anything you do at the mixing board will not eliminate the distortion. On the other hand, many times you can bring out or subdue background noises through equalization. Use your imagination and try out a few things. Thoughtful experimentation can lead to some rewarding results.

Consistency. When working on a shoot or a series of shoots, it is very important to treat your audio track in a consistent manner. Postproduction can turn into a nightmare if you recorded your on-camera narrator with five different microphones at five different locations, which are then edited together in the finished program. This goes for almost every item on the audio list, especially on a multilocation or multiday shoot. Try to keep your levels consistent. Try to keep each person sounding the same from day to day and location to location. Sometimes you may have to use more than one microphone in different locations for the same person. When you do, try to match the sound of the voice as closely as you can. Minor differences can be made up for in postproduction more easily than major differences. If you have ever tried to make the audio track fit together during postproduction and nothing seems to fit, you can relate to this problem. Although it is true that many things can be fixed "in post," it is also true that there is usually neither the time, money, nor energy to do so.

Recording On-Camera Voices

Some video people get involved with audio only while recording on-camera talent. Keeping the above items in mind will help you a great deal. However, you must still decide what type of microphone to use, whether you want a microphone in the shot, what parts of the on-camera portion you will use in the final edited master, etc. Many times the answers to some or all of these questions are determined by someone else, such as your director, boss, client, or talent. When you have a choice, you generally will get the best results with whatever is most comfortable for the talent.

Some of these decisions will be determined by convention. That is, it is conventional to see microphones on stage for a music video, while it is not conventional to see microphones in a dramatic production. All of these things must be considered together. The goal is to get the cleanest voice recording possible while meeting the needs of the production.

If you are recording your on-camera talent in a quiet environment, you can mic the talent a number of ways. You can have the talent hold a microphone if that is in keeping with the total production. You can use a lavalier, either hard-wired or wireless, depending on whether the cable would be seen in the shot. You also can use the traditional film miking technique with a shotgun microphone on a boom. If this one shot is the only place that person is seen in the production, then do whatever is most comfortable for the talent and easiest for you.

If the talent will appear at other times in the production, however, you would want to be consistent throughout, if possible. Then you have to determine the "worst case" or most difficult scene with respect to audio, and mic your talent in that way. However, just because you might need to use a wireless microphone in one of a dozen scenes, it may not be desirable to use the wireless in every scene. If it does not present any problems, then do it, but otherwise do not be afraid to use wireless and wired lavaliers on talent. Do try to make them sound as consistent as you can.

Recording Voice-Overs

Voice-overs are defined here as a voice which does not have to be in lip-sync with on-camera talent. Most of the time this would be a narrator or an offstage voice. It could be someone yelling in the background or a voice on the other end of the telephone. These voices can be recorded on location or in the recording studio during postproduction. Where you record it usually depends on how you handle the shoot. As we will see discussed in the next section, however, the background sound or *presence* is an important consideration. Replacement of voice-over voices during postproduction is usually much easier and faster than for lip-sync material. Your attention while recording voice-overs, other than those mentioned above, should be directed to the delivery of the material, and the timing of the delivery. Sometimes a single second in the length of the delivery can be very important, while other times it does not matter. You need to determine this ahead of time, before the talent arrives.

Dealing with Presence

Presence is defined here as all sounds in the background. Generally, these sounds are unique to a particular location. Pres-

41

ence on a street corner may include people talking, cars passing, kids at play, and people walking on concrete, whereas presence in a hospital hallway may include people walking on tile, a doctor's page, a food cart, and a room door closing. The use of presence, whether recorded on location or in postproduction, is crucial to the quality of a production. Feature-film sound editors will spend days and weeks constructing the appropriate presence for a scene. In a less-than-Hollywood production, presence is usually not noticed when it is there, but definitely is noticed when it goes away or changes. Paying attention to this type of detail in your sound can make an extremely large difference in the effect your production has on the viewers.

The presence needs to fit the scene. However, it does not always need to be recorded at the scene or even on location. The safest way to deal with presence is to try to minimize the presence level on the voice tracks, but at the same time making sure you record enough presence for use during postproduction. Record it at the same levels and with the same equipment you are using for the rest of the scene. Then during postproduction, you can add more of the presence you recorded if you need it. Or you can augment the presence with sounds from libraries of other specific sounds for that location.

Recording Sound Effects

Sound effects (SFX) are a valuable part of many video productions. Recording sound effects usually takes one of three forms. First, there is the recording of the effect as it happens, such as a door closing or a plane flying overhead. Special care must be taken when recording most sound effects. Many effects are percussive and sharply transient in nature; if you try to set levels so that the meter moves to zero, you will probably be in trouble. Most VU meters react relatively slowly; sometimes a percussive sound will barely move them. That's fine—as long as it sounds good when played back. When recording your sound effects during shooting, it is best to use your ears and set the levels to where you want it to sound.

Second, sound effects can be created in the recording studio. In the Hollywood tradition this is called *Foley*, and the recording stage is called a *Foley stage*. This technique is similar to automatic dialog replacement (ADR) in that one or more people watch the visuals and create the sound effects to match the action. A standard Foley stage has many types of surfaces for creating different sounds, as well as other tried-and-true techniques for simulating sounds of all types. This technique is very useful, but a little experience helps a great deal. You can do it yourself, especially when there are only a few effects involved, and you can record directly to video tape or to a multitrack tape deck.

Third, sounds can be substituted for other sounds. For example, the sound of an opening door may be replaced with a Zing! sound. If it is in sync with the door opening, there will be no doubt as to what it is. This is an alternative to using the actual sound, and you may be able to create an atmosphere that would not be possible with the real sound. This trick can be used to call attention to or purposely exaggerate something.

Sometimes the recording of a real effect does not sound enough like the real thing; the microphone might have "heard" it differently than your ears. When this happens you need to find a suitable substitute. The solution may be to record a similar sound, or another sound altogether. If you are able to work with an original music score, the sound effects sometimes can be scored into the music. Although this should not be done all of the time, it can really spice up a production if done tastefully and creatively. Sometimes this is also effective when using library music, if you can make the effect take on a musical nature which fits with the key and the beat of the music.

Chapter 4

Audio in the Video Edit

ed • it \ 'ed- ə t \ *vt* **1** : to prepare or revise for publication **2** : to concatenate electronically various segments of video and audio material into a television program

The classic sweetening process formally begins only after the video edit is complete, but audio tracks built during the video edit are often principal elements of the final soundtrack. In a sense, editing audio in the video suite thus is a part of the track-building phase of sweetening. The typical reader of this book is assumed to be someone involved in television production in some way and therefore familiar with video editing; most of them probably have edited video programs and therefore have edited audio tracks on video tape. However, another segment of the audience may be audio production people to whom editing audio means razor blades and splicing tape. For the interested parties, the next section is a brief review of video editing. Skip it if you like. The sections following that are concerned with issues specific to audio editing and track building during the video edit.

VIDEO EDITING

A television program is made up of many scenes, originally recorded out of sequence, at different times, on different tapes. Piecing these scenes together is video editing. The program is not assembled by physically connecting together the originally recorded scenes, because physically splicing video tape is impractical. The show is made by copying each of the scenes onto a new video tape, head to tail, in program order.

The principle is simple; the machinery to execute it is complex. Recording a lone scene off one tape onto another is easy enough, but to accurately record a second segment such that its beginning matches the desired end of the preceding scene presents the difficulty. The mechanics of video tape recorders dictate that tape must be rolling in order to record a video signal properly. To ensure that the exact beginning of the new scene is recorded at the exact end of the last scene, the source VTR must reach the starting frame of the new scene exactly as the record VTR passes the last frame of the preceding scene. Finally, in order to record a clean transition from the old to the new, both the source VTR and the record VTR must be rolling in sync, i.e., rolling at the same speed with each deck reading the start of each video frame at precisely the same instant. Altogether this amounts to a complex task of synchronizing two machines, a task impossible without sophisticated electronic control circuitry.

So evolved the editing VTR and the edit controller, which share the load of synchronizing machines for editing. To record a scene from a source tape into a precise position in a program tape, the operator specifies the starting frame of the source, the starting frame in the program, and the end of either to the edit controller. The machinery does the rest—rolling both VTRs, aligning the proper source and program frames, synchronizing the video frame boundaries, and enabling and disabling record mode at the specified frames.

Since video tape carries separate signals for the visual and audio portions of the program, duplicating a scene from source tape to program tape requires that both video and audio signals be transferred and recorded. The editing VTRs and controllers provide the ability to record either video or audio independently. Thus, the audio can be laid down either before the visual or after. The desired audio may come from a source other than the source video tape. Since the video and audio signals are completely independent, audio may be sent to the record VTR from a variety of sources—1/4" audio tape, phonograph records, or audio cassettes.

For audio-only edits where the source audio is coming from video tape, operation is the same as for video edits. The edit in and out points are marked on the source and record tapes and the controller executes the edits. On the other hand, if the audio is coming from another device (such as an audio tape recorder), the record VTR may be controlled by the edit controller, but the operator must cue and roll the audio deck. After setting up the edit points on the record VTR (and perhaps dummy edit points on a source VTR) he locates the source material and backs up the source audio tape for a sufficient preroll. To execute the edit, he starts the edit with the edit controller and at the precalculated moment rolls the ATR. If his manual preroll and timing were right, the desired source piece falls into place when the record VTR drops into record. This is often termed *hot rolling* the source.

It is possible—albeit difficult—to create a sweetened audio track using multiple sources and a mixing console in a simple video editing environment. For example, suppose the visual for a particular scene (in an industrial program) about a manufacturing company is a factory machine in operation. The natural audio for the machine is recorded with the video. The narration for the scene is on 1/4" audio tape and the factory environment ambience is recorded on audio cassette. While the edit controller executes an audio/video edit, the operator hot rolls the 1/4" ATR and the audio cassette deck, feeding a mix of the narration, the ambience, and the natural sound from video tape to the record VTR—three layers of audio without multitrack sweetening.

This works, but its limits are rapidly encountered. Imagine that the example program calls for a music bed under the scene, a music bed that begins under the preceding scene and continues under the next scene. This approaches an impossible task with only the tools described thus far.

An *A/B roll editing system* has two source VTRs controlled by the edit controller. The two VTRs are used for dual-source video transitions and video special effects. A dissolve, for example, is made by mixing two rolling video sources; the edit controller must synchronously roll both source VTRs to execute the proper edit. Having two controlled sources can be useful in audio edits. When the edit controller executes a dual-source event such as a dissolve, both source VTRs are rolling from the supposed video transition through to the end of the event. The two rolling sources can be used as two audio sources to be mixed for an audio edit. This system could simplify the preceding example if one of the secondary audio sources were on video tape. If the factory ambience were found on video tape under other factory footage, then the three audio sources could be mixed using a dual-source event and hot rolling only the narration from the 1/4" ATR. These techniques are extremely useful in building audio when there is no option for multitrack sweetening.

The method of frame referencing used by the video editor is critical in planning a sweetening system configuration and the operating methods. As already discussed, SMPTE time code is essential for multitrack sweetening. Video edit controllers that use time code are naturally compatible with sweetening hardware and methods. Other video edit controllers that use the control track signal from video tape as the frame reference place certain restrictions on the methods used for sweetening. A control track editing system in combination with a time code sweetening system will work, but demands special consideration in certain processes.

Without a lengthy discourse on time code (these can be found in other sources), recognize that the essential difference between time code and control track referencing is that time code provides an absolute reference while control track is a relative reference. Attached to every frame of video is a time code number that can be read individually and always remains constant. Control track referencing counts frames from an arbitrary zero point; hence, the number of a particular frame depends on the established zero point and on the accuracy of the counting process. If the reference point changes, as it will any time a tape is removed from the VTR, or if the counter loses or gains a count, as it will from time to time, the reference number of a particular frame will change. The absolute repeatability of time code reference is what allows synchronized program audio to be recorded on a multitrack ATR and later transferred back to video tape in perfect sync.

Editing with a time code system or a control track system is in principle the same. The advantages afforded by time code are accuracy and repeatability. By reading time code, the edit controller knows exactly where the source and record tapes are at every instant and can drive the two VTRs into accurate alignment at the edit point. What is more, knowing the time code numbers means that the exact edit can be repeated accurately over and over, after removing the tapes, on different days, even in different edit systems. Keeping a record of the time code numbers for all of the events in a program allows a program to be re-edited, modified, or entirely rebuilt at a later time. Most time code edit systems provide a method of permanently recording the complete list of time code numbers for a program, usually both in print and in machine-readable form, such as on punched tape or floppy disk. This edit list, either in print or machine-readable media, can be a vital part of sweetening.

Off-line editing is the practice of editing to produce a video sample cut and an edit list. The off-line bay uses 3/4″ or 1/2″ video equipment without fancy frills and effects. The off-line edit is conducted using dubs of the source tapes with duplicate time code. The video edited master produced in the off-line bay is not the finished program, but serves as a representation of the program for editorial evaluation. The edit list is the real product of the off-line bay; when the off-line cut is finished and reworked and perfect, the edit list plus the original field masters are taken to a full-power post house for on-line video mastering. Here the edit controller will read the edit list and will automatically or semiautomatically edit together a polished EM. The off-line/on-line process is adaptable to sweetening as well.

BUILDING TRACKS IN THE VIDEO EDIT

In classic sweetening, the phase formally titled "track building" occurs in the sweetening bay following the video edit and the laydown, but actually the first track or tracks were built in the video edit on one or two channels of the EM. This track is usually a dialog and/or narration track, and it is built in the video edit because it is required as a reference for editing the picture. Even though this track will be transferred to ATR and subjected to further improvement and fixing, it pays to build the track as cleanly as possible the first time.

The concerns in editing a dialog/narration track for laydown are basically the same as when editing an audio track that will not be sweetened. Maintaining continuity of voice level and tonal quality are of supreme importance; the better this is accomplished in this edit, the easier the mix will be. If this becomes an extremely difficult task in the video edit, however, remember to consider the capabilities of the sweetening bay and the efficiencies that might be realized later. For example, suppose that two actors require dramatically different equalization. If only a single equalization channel were available in the video bay, nearly every edit would require changing the EQ parameters. Saving the EQ problem for sweetening would allow splitting the dialog to two separate EQ units—a much more efficient solution.

Presence holes are a demon best dealt with in the video bay. A *presence hole* is a gap in the background noise under dialog or narration, caused when the in point of an audio edit does not match or overlap with the out point of the preceding audio edit, leaving frames or even seconds with nothing recorded. It is a temptation to say that ambient noise, added later, will cover this hole. Sometimes this is true, but sometimes the hole will cause an audible bump in the ambience due to the additive nature of different types of noise. The best plan is to fill the holes in the video edit. It is easier to fill these holes in the video edit because the video in and out points will coincide with the holes and the proper noise to use for filling the hole is generally available on the source material currently in use.

Aside from dialog and narration, other types of audio are occasionally necessary as reference during the video edit. Music for a montage is a perfect example. The music must be laid down on the EM for timing the video cuts and the overall duration. These other audio elements may be incorporated into the EM audio track for layover to the ATR, or they later may be rerecorded directly to the ATR, depending on synchronization considerations. Here the constraints of control track editing come into play.

The principal drawback of control track editing is that events are not accurately repeatable, and therefore tightly synchronized audio elements must be treated in that light. Music under a montage is again a good example. Once the music is recorded on the EM (to cut visuals to), that track of music must be transferred to the ATR because the sync with the visual cuts would be difficult to duplicate without time code. Synchronized dialog or natural sound effects from video tape are a similar case. These must be recorded as the video edit is made. This is not a problem if these synchronized elements are the only audio at the time and therefore can be recorded onto the EM's audio track, to be saved for laydown to the ATR.

The problem arises when two synchronized audio elements must exist simultaneously. Consider the case of a montage, cut to music, wherein some of the visuals have natural sync sound to be mixed with the music. The music is recorded first, but then what happens to the synchronized sound when the video edit is made? In a time code environment—no problem. Save the code numbers and record the sync sound to the ATR later. With control track, the source audio must be recorded with the video or suffer the task of trying to resync later. If the EM is 1″, the second audio track is a solution. On U-matic, though, the second audio channel is likely to be reserved for time code required in the laydown.

This problem of synchronized audio suggests another solution that can, in fact, be a valuable procedure in many operating environments. The solution is to bring the ATR into the video edit. With time code on the EM and with a basic chase-and-follow synchronizer, synchronized audio "bites" can be laid directly to the multitrack as the video edit is made. Such configurations and their operation is discussed further in Chapter 7. The principle is this: With the ATR locked to the EM, many tracks are now available for building audio during the video edit. In fact, all of the track-building process could be performed as the video edit proceeds.

Even those elements normally edited to the VTR could be recorded directly on the multitrack, eliminating the laydown process and saving one generation of audio transfer.

While this reorganization of the system and process progression is the only practical solution for some situations in control track video bays, it also offers interesting options for time code editing environments. With the option of building tracks in the video edit or in postedit sweetening, efficiency factors can be weighed to determine the strategy. For example, synchronized background sound from video tape could be recorded in the video edit or later, using the time code edit list. While editing video though, the source reels are already hung and the material is located. If the process is postponed, an extra price is paid in reel shuffling and cueing time. On the other side, building background presence from loops or laying non-sync music beds is not more efficient in the video mode and could be done later, freeing the video bay for other usage.

Incorporating the synchronizer and ATR into the video edit system places a greater burden on the operator because more manual operations are required. The time saved may be worth the effort; the disruption of the video process may prove this strategy less efficient.

OFF-LINE SWEETENING

How does off-line editing interface with sweetening? Through the edit list, of course. Once again, the exact procedures depend on the editing configuration and whether sweetening will be done in-house or at an outside sweetening bay. Regardless of the exact strategy, it is safe to assume that there is a strong economic motivation to minimize the time spent in the outside video on-line suite and in an outside sweetening bay.

If sweetening as well as video on-lining is done out of house, the best preparation is a comprehensive edit list. The more complete the edit list, the smoother the assembly will proceed. Carefully construct the audio edits to avoid snivits and upcuts that might well go unnoticed in a low-fi off-line room. Create list events to fill presence holes. Plan to do as much audio with time code as possible. The rationale here is that time code assembly, even in the video suite, will be more cost-effective than hot rolling in the sweetening bay. Following this line of thought, separate edit lists for background sync tracks and other time-coded audio could be autoassembled to track two of the EM, or to an on-line ATR in the video suite, to take maximum advantage of the efficiency of autoassembly.

Some sweetening bays, typically Hollywood-style, are built

around video edit controllers such as the CMX 340. In such a case, an off-line edit list can be fed directly to the controller for sweetening. The next generation of synchronizers undoubtedly will be able to read digital edit lists for this purpose. Given a sophisticated synchronizer, even now the edit list could be used to advantage by reentering the code numbers edit by edit. The edit list conceivably could have events for assembly of a dialog track and/or natural sync sound from video tape, plus narration, music, and effects from time-coded audio tape—making the whole track-building process virtually automatic.

Off-line video editing with in-house sweetening is rarely encountered in the world of small-scale productions. We have employed this combination quite creatively and cost-effectively, but the procedure only makes sense in selected circumstances. In this case, most production was originated on U-matic. Time-coded window dubs on Beta cassettes were off-line edited to a U-matic rough cut, producing a complete edit list. The edit list with U-matic source cassettes were then autoassembled at a commercial post house to a 1" EM.

Sweetening was generally performed prior to autoassembly of the final program. After completing the rough cut, the edit list was used in the sweetening configuration to rebuild the dialog and natural synchronized sound tracks from the original field master cassettes to the ATR. Music and effects tracks were built on the ATR in the conventional manner. The mix was sent back to one track of the ATR, then code and mix were transferred to 1/2" 4-track audio tape and carried to the post house for layback prior to the video assembly.

On other occasions, a more conventional progression was followed. Rough cut was followed by autoassembly of the video and a dialog/narration track at the post house. This track was laid down to audio tape and sweetened in-house, returning to the post house for layback of the final soundtrack.

This formula worked because the in-house system could handle the field master cassettes. A program originated on 1" would have presented difficulties, since audio from the field masters could not have been retrieved in-house. Still, the system would have been used in conjunction with additional audio editing in the on-line room. A more common off-line configuration uses U-matic decks for both source and record. Adding a synchronized ATR during the off-line would allow simultaneous track building for greater efficiency. The remainder of the tracks could be built before or after the on-line, depending on the plan for assembly of the dialog/narration track.

The point of these examples is that there are many ways to

go about combining sweetening with video editing, either on-line or off-line, and clever application of available facilities can save time or money. For the production group already set up with off-line editing, addition of sweetening equipment is a much smaller investment with quicker payback than adding on-line video gear.

Chapter 5

Basic Sweetening Hardware

syn • chro • ni • za • tion \ siŋ -krə-nə-' zā-shən \
n **1** : a state wherein events occur together in
time and proceed at exactly the same rate **2** : an exact linkage of audio to an existing video program **3** :
interlock

The introduction presented in the preceding chapters has pointed
out that the process of audio sweetening combines basic techniques from audio and video production, plus additional techniques
particularly cultivated for the purpose of sweetening audio for video.
Similarly, the equipment in a sweetening system is a mix of conventional video and audio postproduction hardware, plus certain
additional elements necessary to bridge the two worlds.

The basic tools of video postproduction are the video tape
recorder and the edit controller; the analogous tools in audio production are the multitrack audio tape recorder and the mixing console. Building and sweetening a complete audio track utilizes both
of these systems. Each processes audio in a different way and for
a different purpose, but the functions are complementary and compatible. Because the electronic signals are compatible, audio tracks
from VTRs may be transferred to ATRs and vice versa; this is of
course essential to allow the use of the features of each system in
producing sound tracks for video programs. The additional require-

ment for these two systems for sweetening, however, is that the two must be synchronized when performing these transfers and also when executing the other stages in the process.

In concept, the requirement of synchronization is not unique. Audio production for other purposes is also subject to synchronization constraints. Audio tracks for multi-image slide presentations must be synchronized; audio production for live events also must be synchronized, but the processes and especially the precision of synchronization are very different for each of these applications. In multi-image, the timing of the visuals is ultimately the more flexible element. When the audio track is complete, the final program for the projector control typically will be adjusted to maintain synchronization with the audio track. During presentation, the projectors are driven by the audio tape recorder. The audio production process is not strictly slaved to the visual program.

In audio production for live events, the audio producers will be cued by the program in progress, but the required precision of synchronization is measured in seconds—well within the realm of human response and easily achieved through direct human control.

Synchronization for sweetening video presents an altogether different problem, driven by two factors. First, the sweetening process begins when the video editing is complete, so the audio production is absolutely slaved to the existing visual program. Second, the accuracy of synchronization required for full-scale sweetening is on the order of hundredths of a second. Combined, these constraints give rise to the special equipment required to perform audio sweetening for video.

The purpose of this chapter is to introduce and discuss the audio sweetening system hardware, including the types of equipment, their functions, and interfaces. As mentioned, this includes VTRs, ATRs, edit controllers, mixing consoles, and peripheral audio processing units—all familiar items in either the video or audio production environment. In addition, the sweetening system includes some devices specifically related to the synchronization function, devices not typically familiar to either the audio or video producer operating individually. Since numerous references are available on the more conventional engineering aspects of audio production in both the pure audio and video environments, the concentration of this chapter will be on the synchronization aspects: the synchronizing devices; the features of the conventional equipment which affect the synchronizing process; and the interrelationships among the components. The more conventional elements of audio and video postproduction will be discussed briefly in order to present a well-rounded picture of the sweetening system.

The configuration and complexity of a sweetening system can vary as much as the configuration of a video editing system or an audio production system. And like the above, sweetening systems do not come prepackaged; a sweetening system is a collection of equipment from different manufacturers which, although intended to work together, must often be interfaced and debugged by the user, postpurchase.

Sweetening Hollywood-style has been mentioned already, and surely those systems represent the state of the art in sweetening technology when precision, fidelity, and productivity are highly valued, and when cost of equipment (both purchase and maintenance) is of minimum concern. For the smaller-scale producer, the first three criteria are certainly important but the last is often the controlling factor. Only recently has a new generation of sweetening-related technology made this process cost-effective for small-scale productions. In building a sweetening system, the choice of equipment depends on the types of programming to be produced, existing postproduction methods, and of course, the budget. Complicating the problem for the small-scale producer is how to begin to build sweetening capabilities, integrating new equipment into an existing postproduction system while planning for expansion in the future.

The producer or engineer must understand how the components of the sweetening system will fit together in terms both of physical interface with the existing postproduction equipment and operational procedures required to complete the job—a systems-level understanding. Toward this end, this chapter focuses on the physical devices, while Chapter 7 addresses the system configurations and associated procedural considerations.

In the preceding discussion of the sweetening process, some idea of the components and their relationships has already been given. Nonetheless, we should start from basic concepts, illustrating the components and their relationships, then continue on to the individual devices.

Figure 5-1 illustrates the essential audio ingredients in the system. The three machines on the left are source machines. For laydown and track building, they supply the raw materials to the multitrack ATR pictured on the right. Ideally, all the audio sources will be routed through the mixing console. The three sources shown here are a U-matic VCR, a 1/4" 2-track ATR, and a phonograph. This is neither the minimum nor maximum set of sources, but will serve as examples for now. The mix process principally utilizes the multitrack and the console. In the layback, the VTR (originally labeled a source machine) becomes the record or destination ma-

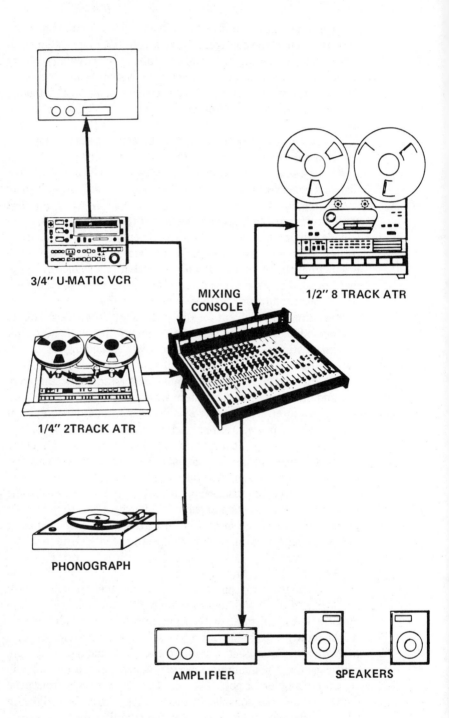

3/4" U-MATIC VCR

MIXING
CONSOLE

1/2" 8 TRACK ATR

1/4" 2TRACK ATR

PHONOGRAPH

AMPLIFIER

SPEAKERS

Fig. 5-1. The principal audio devices in a basic sweetening system.

chine for the final, mixed sound track. The final mandatory audio element is the monitoring system, an amplifier and speakers pictured below the console. This basic audio system is probably well understood, at least in concept, by anyone with some production background either in audio or video.

As shown, this system is not sufficient to perform true sweetening for video. The missing element is synchronization. As previously noted, many of the stages in the sweetening process require high-precision synchronization of the multitrack ATR and the visual program on the VTR. Figure 5-2 expands the previous diagram, adding in a representation of the synchronizing controller. As illustrated here, there are two physical units, the main electronic unit and the operator's console. This is representative of devices on the market called *synchronizers*. The functional differention between the units is that the electronics package performs basic machine control and synchronization, while the console allows the operator to specify parameters and activate auxiliary functions. The synchronizer is an ideal solution to the problem of synchronizing two or more audio or video machines and will be described in more detail later in this chapter. There are other devices for achieving the synchronization and control necessary for sweetening (video edit controllers, for one) or hybrid combinations of edit controllers and synchronizers. The best solution depends on the degree of integration with systems already in place, the planned methods of use, and the budget.

Figure 5-2 represents a basic sweetening system and thus identifies the six fundamental hardware components needed to sweeten. These are:

1) A VTR for picture viewing, audio source for laydown, and destination for layback.
2) Audio source machine or machines for other audio input during track building.
3) A mixing console.
4) A multitrack ATR.
5) Some kind of synchronization/control system.
6) An audio monitoring system.

This basic system can be expanded in every direction, adding more audio sources, additional record machines, and audio processing and effects devices. The additional audio machines may require further synchronization and control capabilities, and maybe a larger mixing console as well.

Figure 5-3 is an illustration of an expanded system. Note the 4-track source ATR, the 16-track ATR locked to the original 8-track

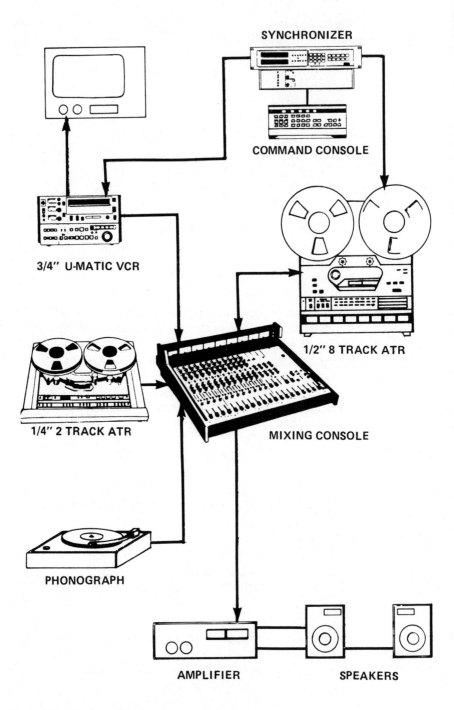

SYNCHRONIZER

COMMAND CONSOLE

3/4″ U-MATIC VCR

1/2″ 8 TRACK ATR

1/4″ 2 TRACK ATR

MIXING CONSOLE

PHONOGRAPH

AMPLIFIER

SPEAKERS

Fig. 5-2. The basic sweetening system with synchronizer control.

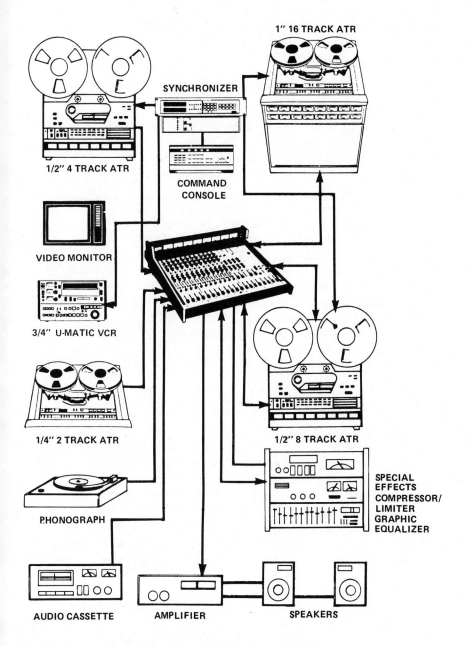

Fig. 5-3. A sweetening system with expanded audio capabilities.

(giving 24-track recording capability), and the outboard compressor/limiter, graphic equalizer, and special effects processor. A system of this magnitude may not be justifiable outside of

Hollywood, but any one of the additional devices might be effective for specific program production needs or operational methods, even in small-scale productions.

TIME CODE

In a discussion of sweetening hardware that concentrates on system synchronization and control, there is a fundamental tool which must be understood before any of these issues can be understood. Almost everyone in the video or audio production industries has encountered this tool in one setting or another: time code.

Why time code is a necessity for sweetening is actually the important question here. What it is and how it works electronically are useful for the engineer to know and may be of interest to the producer, but are not necessary for our purposes. Thorough explanations of time code are available in many sources. Two manufacturer-printed booklets on the subject are *Time Code Handbook* from Datametrics-Dresser Industries, Inc., and *SMPTE/EBU Longitudinal and Vertical Interval Time Code* from EECO, Inc. If you already have a handle on time code, you may want to skip to the next section.

To demonstrate time code, consider yourself about to test a piece of music as a background cue for a video scene. The music is on tape, mounted on your 1/4″ audio deck. For the test, you plan to play the music cue while watching the video and listening to both. First, you cue up the music by rocking the reels, marking the tape with a grease pencil so that you can return to that position to repeat the test, if necessary. It sounds pretty good—but it might be better if the video scene started after the first four bars of the music. Rock the reels and mark the tape again at the end of the first four bars. Line up the mark with the heads, cue the VTR and watch again. Good, but maybe it was better the first way. Try it again returning to the first mark on the music tape. These grease pencil marks allow you to find and resynchronize the audio tape to the video.

If the audio tape had a scale printed on the back, you could write down ruler-like numbers off the scale where the cue points were, rather than making marks on the tape. Then you could return to either cue point number, or a point halfway between, or one quarter of the way between, or even two beats after the early cue—all by interpolating from the two observed numbers.

Time code is an electronic implementation of the printed scale. By encoding the scale as an electronic signal, electronic devices can read and use the code to locate and cue the tape, much the same as a person might read the printed scale to cue the tape manually.

Electronic coding and reading offers an added capability. Because electronic devices can read the code and react much faster, the electronic device has the ability to precisely monitor the speed of the tape deck by continuously reading the code and performing timing comparisons. An individual, reading the printed scale with the tape running, could perform coarse estimates of speed, but could never compare with the accuracy of the electronic code reader.

Time code and the associated electronic reader thus provide two fundamental capabilities: accurate, repeatable identification of positions on a tape and precise, dynamic measurement of tape speed. This much may already have made it obvious how time code fits into the synchronizing of audio and video; if not, the explanation will continue in the section on synchronizers.

Time code is "time" code because of the units of measurement selected for the electronic scale. A scale physically printed on the tape might naturally be calibrated in inches or millimeters, and so might the electronic scale. Using inches or any unit of linear measure carries no natural correspondence to the program material actually being measured, so the originators of the code wisely chose units of time as a more practical measure for the audio or video producer. If a tape is played at normal speed from an arbitrarily chosen starting point, the quantified measure of a particular point on the scale is the time elapsed from the start until that point on the tape reaches the play head. Time is quantified into the normal hours, minutes, and seconds; for the sake of the video community, the seconds are subdivided into frames, corresponding to the 30 frames per second (approximately) of video presentation. Hence, in written or display form, time code commonly appears as

HR:MN:SC:FR

for hours, minutes, seconds, and frames.

The time code format generally used in audio and video production today was standardized by the Society of Motion Picture and Television Engineers (SMPTE) in 1969. This widely accepted standard specifies both the logical and physical implementation of the code, that is, how the numerical time count is translated to binary coding and exactly what electronic signals are used to encode the binary time representations of the magnetic tape. The electronic format was designed to be compatible with the characteristics of standard audio recording channels, allowing time code to be recorded on any audio channel of a multitrack audio or video tape.

Recently several other methods of recording and reading time code have been developed especially for video use, partially to preserve the use of the second audio track for true audio; these methods are *vertical interval time code* and *embedded video address track*. The details of the formats and electronic standards are presented in other references, including the SMPTE specification and the above-mentioned booklets.

SYNCHRONIZERS

Since synchronization and machine control are the key features which make sweetening different from audio or video production alone, the synchronizer must become the focus of this chapter. A synchronizer is basically a device which controls the play speed of an audio or video tape deck to keep it synchronized with another tape deck. In the most basic configuration there are two tape decks, audio or video, or one of each. The synchronizer is electronically connected so that it has the ability to activate the motion of one or both of the machines. The tapes in both of the machines are time-coded and the time code output from each is fed to the synchronizer.

In such a two-machine configuration, one deck is called the *master* and the other is the *slave*; the master may or may not be controlled by the synchronizer but the slave deck is always controlled by the synchronizer. The function of the synchronizer is to make the slave follow the master. The time code from the master tells the synchronizer where the master is or is going. By electronically activating the motion of the slave deck, the synchronizer drives the slave, monitoring its time code until the slave is at the same place as the master, i.e., until the time code readings from the two decks are equivalent. The basic master-slave configuration is illustrated in Fig. 5-4. Note that the master only supplies time code to the synchronizer, while the synchronizer both reads code from and exercises full control over the slave.

Assume that both the master and the slave decks are stopped and that the synchronizer has read a valid time code from each of its current position. (This implies that each has recently moved into position at proper speed, with synchronizer activated, but disregard this for the moment.) From the value of the time code readings, the synchronizer determines whether the slave is ahead of or behind the master. If the slave is ahead, i.e., the slave time code is numerically greater than the master, then the slave must move backward to approach the position of the master. The synchronizer will then issue the required electronic signal to set the slave deck into rewind. As the deck rewinds, the time code from the slave decreases, drawing closer to the master time code position. When the slave code is sufficiently close to the master, the synchronizer

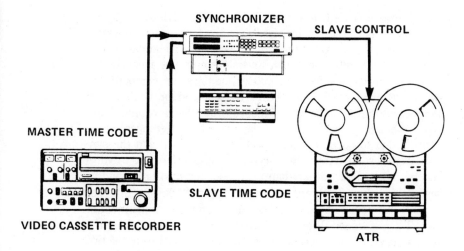

SYNCHRONIZER

SLAVE CONTROL

MASTER TIME CODE

SLAVE TIME CODE

VIDEO CASSETTE RECORDER

ATR

Fig. 5-4. Master-slave configuration with time-code-only master.

issues a stop command and ideally the slave comes to rest at the same position as the master.

On the other hand, if the slave is behind the master—indicated by slave time code being less than master time code—the slave must move forward to match the master. Here the synchronizer has the option of moving the deck with a play command or a fast-forward command. Barring operating mode restrictions, the choice is made based on the distance from the slave's current position to the desired position. If the distance to be moved is small, the synchronizer will put the deck in play; if the distance exceeds some preset criterion, the synchronizer will use fast-forward. Again, once the deck is moving the synchronizer monitors the advancing position of the tape and stops the deck when it is aligned with the master. Neglecting the details of accurately finding the exact stopping position, this is the essence of the synchronizer's positioning function.

More difficult is the job of following a moving master. The real use of the synchronizer is in driving the slave to follow the master when the master is in play mode. This is the true synchronizing function that keeps audio playing on an ATR "in sync" with video playing on a VTR. The necessity for synchronization arises from the fact that an audio tape deck will not play at an absolutely accurate speed for long periods of time. If two decks are put into play mode at the same moment, starting from the exact same position on their respective tapes, the small variance in deck speeds will put them out of sync after a relatively short time. As the video folks know, VTRs are different. Because VTRs have servo systems which lock to external sync, two video decks started at the same

63

video frame will remain in sync for indefinite periods.

Conceptually, the synchronizer's process for following the playing master is similar to the process for locating to a stationary position, but executed frequently and in small steps. The synchronizer repeatedly reads code from the master and the slave, compares the two to determine whether the slave is ahead or behind, and generates the motion control signal to bring the slave into alignment. When the two decks are in play mode the differences in tape position due to speed variance will be very small, and the synchronizer must have the ability to correct these differences by varying the play speed, rather than using fast forward or rewind as described earlier. The defines a requirement for the synchronizer to ATR interface: There must be a means for fine adjustment of the ATR play speed through external electronic control from the synchronizer. If the synchronizer, upon reading code from the two decks, finds that the slave is slightly behind the master, the synchronizer sends the signal to increase the speed of the slave. Conversely, if the code shows the slave to be ahead of the master, the appropriate signal is sent to slow the slave, allowing the master to catch up.

With the master in play mode, the synchronizer will continually attempt to match the slave's play speed to the master, thereby minimizing the difference in the time code. Of course, it is impossible to exactly match the speeds of the two decks, for only through the detection of time code differential or error can the synchronizer adjust the slave's speed properly. Today's synchronizers are capable of controlling the slave speed to maintain extremely accurate synchronization. The accuracy of synchronization is measured in one-hundredths of a frame, called *subframes*; translated into time, this is 0.00033 second. Most modern synchronizer specifications claim the ability to hold sync within less than one subframe. When the master is playing and the slave is successfully following—holding sync within some predetermined threshold—the slave is said to be "locked." As long as the master continues to play and the time code is not interrupted, the slave will remain synchronized or locked to the master.

How does the synchronizer do all this? Inside nearly every synchronizer is a microprocessor, much like the microprocessor in a desktop or personal computer. The microprocessor is supported by electronic circuits that assist in reading time code, in sending the remote control signals to the decks, and similar physical functions. The essence of the synchronizer's power is in the programs which guide the microprocessor. Stored in hardware memory inside the synchronizer are the programs that govern what actions the microprocessor executes for given sets of operating conditions and inputs. For example, in the programs are the rules that tell the microprocessor to compare the time code of the master to the time code of the slave and, if the code of the slave is lower, to send a signal to the slave deck that will increase the play speed. As one might imagine, the programs in today's synchronizers are quite extensive in order to allow these devices to perform the sophisticated functions they do. Figures 5-5 and 5-6 show two typical modern synchronizers.

Building the synchronizer around a programmable microcomputer offers other advantages as well. Such an intelligent device is capable of altering its behavior by changing numeric parameters rather than making physical adjustments. New functions for the synchronizer are implemented by writing new programs for the microprocessor; with little or no hardware modification, the new functions can be installed in existing machines simply by exchanging the program memory component. Similarly, customized versions of a machine may be created through custom programs. Through built-in communication capability, such an intelligent device can operate in conjunction with other devices to multiply their overall capabilities.

In the course of normal usage the master will be played for a

Fig. 5-5. Cipher Digital synchronizer. The upper unit is a Shadow synchronizer module and the lower unit is the electronic chassis for the Softouch control console. The Shadow contains synchronizer, LTC readers, and serial interface for external communications.

Fig. 5-6. Adams-Smith Synchronizer. The five modules of this System 2600 are, from left to right: power supply, LTC generator, LTC reader, synchronizer, and serial interface. The serial interface allows external devices such as command consoles or a computer to communicate with each of the modules.

time, then cued and played again, or cued to another spot and played from there. When the master stops playing and begins to slow, the synchronizer (unless operationally inhibited) switches to another mode of operation, often called the *chase mode*. In the chase mode, the synchronizer uses fast-forward and rewind motions of the slave to rapidly follow the master. The synchronizer remains in chase mode until it detects that the master is once again in play mode. Then, when the slave comes into the vicinity of the master tape position, the synchronizer reverts to variable play speed synchronizing. At first the error between the master and slave will be greater than the lock criterion and slave will still be "chasing," although in play mode. Controlling the slave's play speed, the synchronizer drives the slave closer and closer to alignment with the playing master until the time code difference falls below the lock criterion, and the decks are again synchronized.

Under this dual-mode control scheme, the slave follows the master wherever it goes, at whatever speed, striving to lock whenever the master is playing. The producer or engineer works as if he has only one machine, operating the master while the slave follows. When the master is a VTR and the slave is a multitrack

ATR, the union of VTR, synchronizer, and ATR acts like the ideal sweetening machine—a tape deck with video and four or eight audio channels.

Now that you have a basic understanding of the operations of the synchronizer, some of the technical details require further clarification. First, the electronic time code signal recorded on tape cannot be read by the electronic readers when the tape is traveling at high speed. Just as recorded music or voice rises in pitch when a tape is played faster than normal speed, the frequency of time code signal increases with increasing tape speed. At play speed the base frequency of time code is 2400 Hz; at ten times play speed, the base frequency is 24,000 Hz, which is beyond the upper limit of reproduction of the playback amplifiers in most tape decks. Additionally, most tape decks lift the tape off the play head when the tape is winding at high speed. Without time code available when a tape deck is in high-speed mode, the synchronizer must have another means of monitoring tape travel.

Most audio tape decks supply to the external interface a signal called the *tach pulse*. This signal line issues one pulse for every unit of tape travel at any speed. For example, if the deck issues 15 tach pulses per second at a play speed of 15 ips, each pulse indicates that the tape has moved 1 inch or 1/15 of a second in time, equivalent to two frames of time code measure. As tape speed increases, the rate of the tach pulses increases; regardless of speed, each pulse tells the synchronizer that the tape has advanced two frames of time code. Tach pulses are active in forward or reverse motion, but another signal is required to alert the synchronizer to the direction of tape travel. Based on the direction signal, the synchronizer either increments or decrements its tape position counter for each tach pulse. The tach pulses are not absolutely accurate, as is the time code, but serve well to update the tape position estimate in fast motion until code can be read again at normal speed.

With VTRs there is no tach pulse, but in its place there is a pulse derived from the tape that serves exactly the same purpose. In U-matic VTRs, for example, this is the *control track pulse*.

In light of this fact, Fig. 5-4 could be misleading, since it shows the synchronizer receiving only time code from the master. Knowing that time code cannot be read in high-speed tape shuttle, this configuration has limitations. If the master uses fast-forward or rewind, the synchronizer will be unable to read or estimate the master position and can only hold the slave idle until time code is again readable. At that point the master may have moved far from the slave position and the user must wait for the slave to relocate. If the master is a VTR which is most often cued or relocated using the search-with-picture mode (at less than ten times play speed), and if the synchronizer has a high-speed code reader, then the synchronizer will almost always know where the VTR is. This may be an entirely adequate configuration; otherwise, a more elaborate interface to the master machine is required.

To be useful in a variety of environments, serving a variety of applications, the synchronizer must be able to control many types of tape decks, both ATRs and VTRs, in many models from many manufacturers. These decks all will have similar features and conform to a minimum set of requirements that allow the synchronizer to exercise effective external control, but beyond these similarities the various machines have many individual characteristics which affect the control mechanics of the synchronizer.

In the first place, the physical interfaces are different. The types of signals input and output through the remote control port are different for each machine. The synchronizer manufacturer deals with this by providing a unique interface for each type of tape deck to be connected.

Once the physical interface is operational, the synchronizer must cope with variations in control characteristics and machine dynamics. The term *control characteristics* refers to the way the deck responds to the control signals sent to it. For example, if the synchronizer sends a voltage to the variable speed input, at what speed does the deck play? Or, what is the nominal rate of tach pulses sent when the machine is at specified play speed? *Machine dynamics* are the characteristics of the machine's motions attributed to physical and electronic features. For example, when sent a fast-forward pulse, how fast does the deck accelerate to full speed and what is the maximum speed? Or, when given a stop signal, what is the rate or profile of deceleration? These characteristics all affect the way in which the synchronizer controls the deck. The synchronizer must be tuned to match the deck characteristics in order to achieve optimum performance.

Since synchronizers are microprocessor-based devices and the programs of the processor govern the control strategies, most of the tuning is realized through changing numeric parameters in the programming. In some synchronizers, the processor is capable of determining the proper values for some of these control parameters, of learning about the characteristics of the attached machine. Otherwise the parameters must be set using buttons or switches or potentiometer adjustments.

Expanding the interface for the master machine to include tach and direction signals leads directly to the next level of system configuration, the *master-slave with controlled master*. This arrangement employs a full control interface between the synchronizer and the master deck, ATR or VTR, and some form of operator command console. The interface to the master gives the synchronizer the ability to initiate motion of the master as well as read its position. The operator console provides a means for the operator to direct the operation of the synchronizer, such as requesting functions other than simple slave-follows-master, entering edit data, and selecting operating parameters. Figure 5-7 illustrates this configuration.

The types of commands available through a typical operator console begin with direct machine control. Much like the remote control units available for most multitrack ATRs, various buttons on the console duplicate the functions of the play, record, fast-forward, rewind, and stop buttons on the tape deck itself. As feedback to the operator, the console will generally have a time code display, which is a digital, numeric readout indicating the time code position of each of the attached machines. The console also will have a numeric keypad or some equivalent means of entering time code numbers. A deck may be commanded to an absolute position on a tape by entering the desired time code location and GOTO-type command.

Through other console controls the operator may enable or disable the synchronizing functions. The synchronizing typically is disabled at start-up; each machine is "free" and will only move when activated through the direct machine motion buttons. When ready to begin synchronized play, the operator presses the appropriate button on the console and the synchronizer takes control

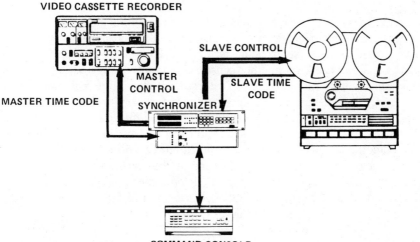

Fig. 5-7. Master-slave configuration with controlled master and operator command console.

of the slave, directing it to follow the master. In selecting synchronization, the operator usually has several choices of modes, including *absolute lock* and *loose* (or *phase*) *lock*. Other variables include the operating strategy in case of loss of lock: The synchronizer may attempt to relock with maximum haste, with or without the use of fast forward and rewind; attempt to relock gradually, using only slight speed variations; or continue to match the master speed without returning to absolute synchronization. And these are not the only options; the various manufacturers have differing implementations, each attempting to provide maximum flexibility for the user.

In the process of synchronization described earlier, the synchronizer reads time code from two tapes and drives the slave machine to exactly match the time code of the master. In practice, there are requirements to synchronize two tapes which have parallel program material but different time code. As long as the time code on each program is continuous, however, there will be a constant differential in the time code values of any two synchronous points of the two tapes. The difference in the time code values is called the *offset* and is numerically computed as slave time code minus master time code. Given a value for offset, the synchronizer can perform master-slave synchronization for tapes with dissimilar time code. The case where the master and slave codes exactly match is actually a subset of this more general case; for matched time code the value of the offset is

$$00{:}00{:}00{:}00.$$

The operator console provides the means of entering an offset other than zero. Using numeric keys, the operator may specify an exact value for the offset from master to slave. This offset number may not always be known; other console features are provided to assist in dealing with these cases. Features such as marking points on the fly, slow retard and advance, and offset capture each have application in synchronizing dissimilar time code material.

The next set of console features are the edit control capabilities. Through the interface, the synchronizer can force a deck into and out of the record mode. Through the console, the synchronizer can be made to set one deck into record mode on a specific time code cue. Using this, in conjunction with offset synchronization, the synchronizer will perform frame-accurate audio edits in much the same way as a video editor.

Finally, layered above all of these functions, the more sophisticated consoles include programmable features. Much like a personal computer, certain keys may be assigned to perform sequences of the aforementioned operations—playing the decks, reading time code, calculating offsets, etc. Using these programmable features, the user can customize the console for any exotic application or operating procedure at hand.

Each of the synchronizer manufacturers offers one or more models of operator console to provide these functions (Figs. 5-8 and 5-9). Various models from a single manufacturer may be differentiated by subsets of functions offered, or by general level of sophistication. Basic offerings may include only direct machine control and operating parameter input, while a complementary model may offer editing and programmable sequence functions. In each case, another console is a simple modular addition to the primary synchronizer unit.

Modularity is made possible by the microprocessor and (borrowing from computer terminology) a "distributed processing" design. The brain of the synchronizer is a microcomputer capable of executing a collection of functions required for and related to synchronizing two tape decks. This microcomputer is also provided with a communication channel to external devices. This is generally

Fig. 5-8. Operator command console for the Cipher Digital Softouch. The 12 keys at the left are a numeric pad for time code and data entry; the remaining keys select operating modes, activate direct machine control, enter edit parameters, and build complex loop sequences. The numeric display reads out machine time codes, programmed loop data and special messages (courtesy Cipher Digital).

Fig. 5-9. The Sony AVS-500 Sync Master includes both synchronizer electronics and operator command console (courtesy Sony Corporation).

an asynchronous serial data interface, either RS-232, RS-422, or current loop. Through this communication channel, the synchronizer's microcomputer can receive commands to execute built-in library functions such as to play the master tape deck or disable the master-slave mode. Upon request over the channel, the microcomputer can send data out to an external device, data such as the time code read from a tape deck.

The operator's console is simply an external device, communicating with the synchronizer through the communication channel. This means that the console is quite independent of the synchronizer, and at the same time means that the console is more than just a few buttons and LED displays, that the console must have its own intelligence. So the console itself is another microprocessor-based device using its intelligence to respond to the operator buttons, compose and transmit commands to the synchronizer, receive data from the synchronizer, and manipulate the displays. It is the intelligence of the console microprocessor that performs the higher-level functions such as time code offset calculations and programmable or looping sequences. This structure allows the console device to be endowed with as few or as many functions as desired without requiring any changes within or placing excessive burden upon the synchronizer.

This distributed design and the public nature of the communication channel makes it possible for devices other than the manufacturer's console to communicate with the synchronizer and thereby control the synchronizer as a console would. A natural candidate for controlling a synchronizer is a personal computer; this will be discussed further in Chapter 7.

AUDIO TAPE RECORDERS

The video producer turning his attention to audio sweetening for the first time may have had little hands-on experience with multitrack audio tape recorders but by now has a good concept of the functions and service of the ATR in the audio sweetening environment. Those with audio production background and an intimate knowledge of ATRs will probably want to skip to the next section, since this section is aimed at the video side of the audience. The goal is not to train audio engineers but to present a few of the significant facts about audio tape decks that will help round out the total picture of audio sweetening system hardware. While this information will not be enough to allow the producer to single-handedly select and install an ATR for his in-house sweetening use, it should make him aware of the issues and problems that the engineer faces in selection and installation, as well as the physical characteristics that enhance and constrain the uses of the unit in everyday production.

To begin, let's establish a basic overview of the ATR as a system made up of several subsystems, each responsible for a separate phase of the device's overall operation. Figure 5-10 is an illustration of the visible physical elements and their relations to the electronic subsystems within the machine.

In principle, the ATR is usually executing two rather independent tasks. The first and foremost is to record and play back electronic audio signals to and from magnetic tape. The three heads pictured in the center of the deck are the transducers that actually convert the electronic signals to magnetic fields and vice versa. The heads—called the *erase head*, the *record head*, and the *repro head*—are connected to the record/play electronics which perform the intermediate signal processing between the heads and the actual input and output jacks. These electronics also drive the meter display of the incoming or outgoing signal levels.

Transporting the magnetic tape is the other fundamental task of an ATR. Anyone who has operated a tape recorder of any type knows that there are at least two modes of tape motion, one for playback and record and another for rapidly transporting the tape to a desired location. To reproduce audio information accurately, it must be recorded and replayed at identical speeds. Moving the tape at a constant or precisely controlled speed is the job of the *capstan, capstan motor,* and *capstan electronics.* The capstan electronics are responsible for maintaining an exact speed of the tape by driving the capstan motor. These electronics sense the speed of the turning motor and adjust the driving signal to keep the speed equal to a reference. This subsystem of capstan, motor, electronics, and speed sensing mechanism is called the *capstan servo system,* with *servo* implying accurate control, usually through the use of sensing mechanisms and feedback loops.

The other mode of tape transport, including at minimum rewind and fast-forward functions, is handled by the *reel motors,* the *reel mechanics,* and the *reel electronics.* To move the tape rapidly forward, for example, the lead reel motor must pull on the tape and the trailing reel motor must resist slightly to keep the tape taut. Until the latest generation of ATRs, this has been accomplished with motors, mechanical brakes and linkages, and simple electronics. Now, more sophisticated reel motion control systems using microprocessors and digital electronics (and fewer mechanical components) are capable of more efficient control with additional features. Microprocessor control systems can more accurately control tape speed and tape tension in fast-forward and rewind. They will maintain a more accurate tape position counter display and can automatically reposition the tape to one or two selected cue points. Some have a bidirectional, medium-speed "spooling" mode to perform constant-tension tape winding. This minimizes print-through in storage.

The two boxes in Fig. 5-10 labeled "user interface" and "external interface" give and take control commands and information from the local operator and a remote control device. Each interface communicates with the central control logic, which coordinates the actions of the other units. This central logic section, usually another microprocessor, initiates and monitors the activities of the other subsystems. For example, when the operator pushes the play button, the microprocessor receives an indication of this from the user interface. If current status allows playing to begin, the microprocessor sends a signal to the capstan servo to play the tape, another signal to the record/play electronics to enable the playback amplifiers, and another signal to light the play indicator.

Simple enough . . . but now suppose that the operator presses

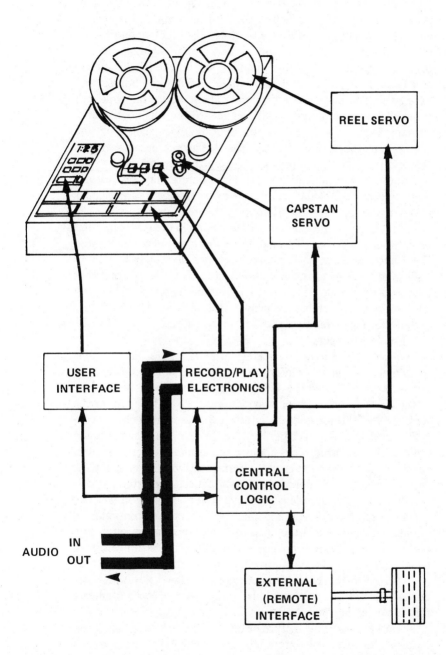

Fig. 5-10. The internal functional elements of an ATR.

the rewind button while the tape is still playing. The microprocessor is so signaled by the user interface, but it knows that the deck is currently playing. Before activating the reel motors, the microprocessor terminates the play mode by sending the appropriate signals to the subsystems to turn off the playback electronics, release the capstan pinch roller, activate the brakes, and extinguish the play indicator light. Then, when the tape has stopped, rewind is initiated with signals to the reel control subsystem. At the end of the rewind, the tape disengages from the lead reel and the tension idler is released. The microprocessor sees this and tells the reel subsystem to stop the rewind.

Audio tape decks did all these things before microprocessors, so who needs them? Quite simply, the microprocessors are cheaper to buy and to operate. Anything that the microprocessor does in today's ATR certainly could have been done in the past, but often at significant expense. The microprocessor and other integrated electronic devices replace volumes of other electronics and eliminate numerous mechanical components. The results are lower manufacturing costs, smaller and lighter packages, lower energy consumption, and greater reliability. All of these contribute to a high-performance multitrack ATR, at a manageable cost for the small-scale producer.

One constraint to be considered carefully in selecting the ATR is the machine control or interface. To establish and maintain sync between the ATR and the VTR, the ATR must be controlled by either an edit controller or a synchronizer. The first concern is whether the ATR provides the interface for external or remote control. Actually, it would be hard to find a professional-grade multitrack ATR which does not have some sort of external control interface. The most basic remote interface allows activation of play, record, fast-forward, and rewind; beyond these, the external interface provides for variable control over the play speed in order to synchronize. Most often, the interface accepts a continuously variable dc voltage and the deck regulates the play speed in proportion to the voltage. Alternately, the ATR accepts an FM signal, usually a logic-level square wave, and the deck regulates the play speed in proportion to the frequency of that signal. An ATR without some provision for external play speed control is not a candidate for a sweetening system.

Another important feature of the ATR interface is tach pulse output. The tach pulse output indicates the distance and speed of tape movement; one pulse is issued for each (arbitrary) unit of tape motion. As described previously, a synchronizer or edit controller uses time code to locate positions on the tape exactly and to control play speed, but when the deck is in fast-forward or rewind the tape is moving so fast that reading time code is not practical. In fast-wind modes, the synchronizer counts the tach pulses to approximate the tape position. As with play-speed control, almost any ATR considered for a sweetening system will have some variety of tach pulse output.

Though similar in function, the connectors, signal protocols, and voltage levels of each ATR's external interface are different; thus, each requires a very specific cable and/or circuits and/or software in the controlling device. Edit controller and synchronizer manufacturers offer standard interfaces for the more popular types of ATR. Synchronizers generally offer a greater variety of ATR interfaces, since they have grown up in the audio environment. For older or more obscure types of ATRs, there may be ways to interface to a synchronizer if the ATR allows external control. Since most synchronizers present a very flexible interface with extensive documentation, an engineer can often adapt the pair to play together. If, on the other hand, the goal is to control the ATR directly with an edit controller, choose an ATR that is supported by the edit controller manufacturer, because their interfaces are not so readily adaptable.

VIDEO TAPE RECORDERS

The third principal component in the sweetening system is the video tape recorder. The VTR plays three distinct roles in the sweetening process: It is a source for dialog and natural sound; it supplies the visual reference during track building and mixing; and finally, it is the destination for the final mix track. For readers from the video realm, video tape recorders are familiar friends and their functions in sweetening are analogous to similar functions in video tape editing. As discussed previously, in the sweetening process the sound and picture reside on different machines, the ATR and the VTR. The two must be played synchronously while sweetening the audio. Incorporating a VTR into such a process focuses attention on several features of the VTR—those features which contribute to synchronizing the ATR and the VTR. In certain ways it is useful to think of the VTR as simply a 2-track ATR.

The fundamental element in synchronizing is time code; the video tape must be time-coded in order to be synchronized. The video tape very likely will be time-coded for the video edit, but if the video edit is performed with a control track editor, eventually the tape must be coded for the sweetening process. On the typical U-matic VTR, this dictates that one of the audio tracks must be held free for the time code, leaving only one track for the audio program. In other situations, two audio tracks will be available, such as with 1″ VTRs, the Sony series of U-matics with dedicated address track, or with vertical interval time code.

Using one audio track of a standard U-matic VTR for time code may present one possible difficulty in certain operating modes. When the VTR is operated in scan or shuttle mode, the audio electronics will not accurately reproduce the time code if the scan speed exceeds three to five times play speed. In a system where the synchronizer is used to make an ATR follow a VTR in code-only mode, the synchronizer cannot follow the VTR without valid time code. This does not preclude the use of this configuration, but it makes the operation more awkward and less efficient.

As tape speed increases, the frequency of the audio signals picked up by the playback head increases; when that frequency exceeds the upper limit of the frequency response of the playback amplifier, the output is no longer distinguishable as valid time code. The playback electronics must have a wider bandwidth to pass the higher frequencies. By altering the characteristics of the playback electronics, time code can be reproduced at higher scan speeds. Often such a modification is made for VTRs used in time code editing systems. Depending on the normal operating configuration, a wideband modification to the VTR for high-speed time code reading may be quite valuable for use in sweetening.

In most cases, the VTR will be under control of the synchronizer or edit controller during the sweetening process. The specific configuration of the system will depend upon the equipment available, the applications, and the preferred methods of operation. For simple sweetening jobs, it may be entirely adequate to drive the VTR manually, using its panel controls. In other situations requiring precise editing from video sources to the multitrack ATR, the VTR must be under control of a synchronizer or edit controller.

As with ATRs, a synchronizer must be specifically interfaced to a type of VTR; most synchronizers can be interfaced to many of the popular types of VTRs. The variety of synchronizer-to-VTR interfaces is not as great as synchronizer-to-ATR interfaces because the synchronizer originated as a tool for audio production. In selecting components for a system, the potential for interface between the synchronizer and the VTR must be examined. If, on the other hand, the planned system centers around an installed video edit controller, the interface to the VTR is already in place.

Audio considerations in selecting a VTR for sweetening are rarely a significant factor. In the first place, within a class of VTRs (U-matics, for example), the audio performance of all VTRs is roughly equivalent because the limits are imposed by track size and tape speed. And second, the choice of a VTR probably will be governed by higher-priority criteria such as picture quality, interface to editor, and budget—leaving audio characteristics little influence on the decision.

Chapter 6

Audio Hardware Considerations

au • dio hard • ware \ ȯd-ē-ō ꞌ här-dwar \ *n* the   half
of the equipment in a sweetening bay that is devoted to
making all the right sounds go into all the right places

Now that we have an understanding of time code and synchronizers,
this chapter will be devoted to a discussion of the audio hardware
required for the audio sweetening process. The "small-scale" audio
hardware used for this type of audio sweetening has evolved from
the "low-end" recording industry. Since the mid-1970s, companies
such as TASCAM, Otari, and Yamaha have been developing and
marketing multitrack equipment for recording environments
smaller than the typical "large-scale" recording studio intended for
the production of record albums. These companies, recognizing the
market niche for lower-cost, high-performance equipment, have developed and refined a broad range of machines that have brought
multitrack recording capability within the range of aspiring recording artists who wish to produce demo material, etc., in order
to secure larger recording contracts. Many a recording artist got
started in his or her living room, building track after track on a
1/4″ 4-track ATR in an attempt to attract major record label backing. Some of these tunes, recorded in these environments, have
made it to actual pressings.

CHOOSING AN ATR

In the initial design of your sweetening facility, one of the first considerations is selecting the multitrack ATR and the number of tracks—four, eight, or sixteen (Fig. 6-1). Although 24-track machines are available, typically they are out of the price range of most small-scale sweetening environments. Beyond the basic economic considerations, there are several factors that affect the choice of machines.

The first absolute requirement is that the ATR have a variable-speed capstan servo system to allow synchronization, as discussed in Chapter 5.

In selecting an ATR for use in a video sweetening system, there are several characteristics of the deck to be considered in light of the expected use and performance of the sweetening system as a whole. The most fundamental question is the tape format, that is, the physical tape size and number of tracks. Tape size ranges from 1/4" to 2", with track count ranging from 2 to 32. Some tape sizes are available with different track layouts; for example, 1/2" tape can be recorded in 2-, 4-, 8-, or even 16-track formats. Advances in tape head fabrication and record/playback electronics are allowing more tracks to be recorded on smaller tape while maintaining

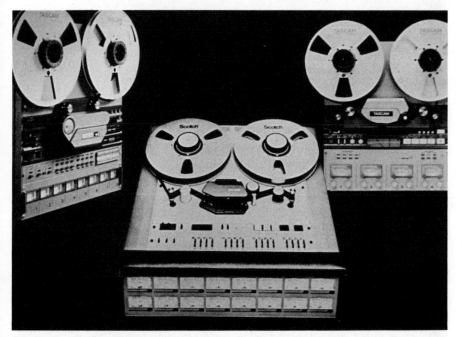

Fig. 6-1. The first equipment decision to make in building an audio sweetening bay is whether to purchase a 4-track, 8-track, or 16-track ATR (courtesy TASCAM).

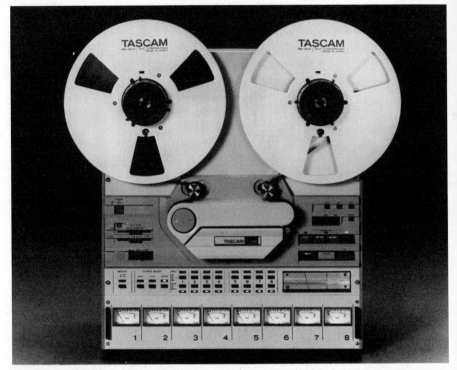

Fig. 6-2. The TASCAM 58 is a 1/2" 8-track ATR designed to be interfaced with synchronizers and edit controllers. It offers the price/performance ratio commensurate with sweetening small-scale productions (courtesy TASCAM).

high-fidelity audio characteristics. The 1/2" 8-track ATR and, more recently, the 1/2" 16-track are examples of these (Figs. 6-2, 6-3, and 6-4).

Weighing the various tape formats together with audio performance specifications, plus other machine features, makes limited-budget ATR selection a tough decision. In sweetening for video, the number of tracks on the tape often takes priority over audio performance. Since the final product is usually distributed on 3/4" or 1/2" video cassette and is heard through the small speaker on a TV set, the absolute quality of the audio signal is not perceptible. However, the content is. That is to say, while the quality of the sound is not reproduced, the elements of the track will all be present. Narration, dialog, music, effects, and ambience will all come through even the small TV speaker. So the video producer is more likely to select an ATR with more tracks, even at a small sacrifice in audio specifications. Note that today's ATRs, even those with lesser specs, are still high-fidelity machines, well beyond the quality of the distribution or reproduction media.

From previous chapters it must be clear that four tracks is a bare minimum for sweetening and will often require submixes to combine all the desired elements. Eight tracks are usually enough for small-scale productions. Sixteen tracks and up may be required for network TV productions, but rarely will be necessary for industrial or educational programs. Not by coincidence, there is a new generation of 1/2" 8-track ATRs that fit perfectly into this level of sweetening system. The TASCAM models 48 and 58 and the Otari model 5050 8-track are examples. Before these machines, the two prime candidates were 1/2" 4-track or 1" 8-track, neither of which matches the value of the 1/2" 8-track in terms of price-performance ratio or dollars-per-track.

Often an 8-track provides barely enough channels, especially if you are doing stereo or dual-language mixes. If you have one or two dialog tracks plus narration, are doing music segues, and have background presence and sound effects, under many conditions you will have used six or seven tracks and still need code on the eighth. On a cable TV program recently produced by the authors, the track assignments were as follows:

Fig. 6-3. Fostex markets a 1/2" 16-track recorder that reportedly was designed for interfacing capabilities with synchronizers, in addition to having optional built-in noise reduction (courtesy Fostex).

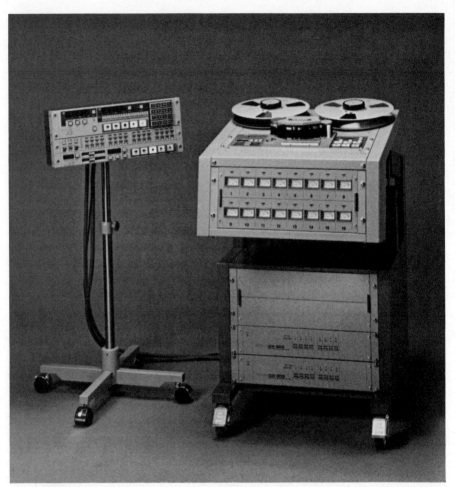

Fig. 6-4. TASCAM has recently introduced the MS-16, its second-generation 1″ 16-track ATR, also designed to be interfaced with synchronizers (courtesy TASCAM).

1) Dialog
2) Production audio
3) Primary music
4) SFX (both 3 and 4 switch)
5) Presence/crowd loops
6) English mix
7) Music/SFX mix
8) Code

With a 16-track machine it is much more difficult to use up the tracks unless you are editing a music video and have to mix down music masters, in which case you may need two interlocked machines (Fig. 6-5).

For many years the film industry has had a standard of "three-striping," which was derived from three actual magnetic stripes on magnetic film: one dedicated to dialog, another to music, and the third to effects. Each mix channel would be recorded to its individual channel and stripe on the record unit. This standard is ideal for 4-track machines, especially when various language versions of a given show may be required for foreign distribution. Additionally, stereo mixes are also well suited to 4-tracks; by recording a stereo mix left and right to channels one and two, with code on track four, track three can be left as a guard band.

Typical prices for ATRs, briefly, are about $3000 for 4-tracks, about $6000 for 8-tracks, and about $10,000 for 16-tracks.

At The Visual Communications Group, Inc., we have three ATRs: a very old Teac 7030 1/4" 2-track, an Otari 5050 series Mark III 1/2" 4-track, and a TASCAM 58 1/2" 8-track. The combination of these machines provides adequate track building and mixing capability, as well as compatibility with the outside world in the 1/2" 4-track and 1/4" 2-track formats.

Concerning traditional audio specifications, there are more authoritative sources than this book for tips on evaluating general ATR audio performance characteristics. The relative importance

Fig. 6-5. At Hollywood-scale facilities it is not uncommon to interlock multiple 24-track recorders for very complex shows, especially concerts to which live music tracks must be conformed.

of these specs in choosing an ATR depends on the variety of your applications, but for an audience listening through a typical television speaker, it would be difficult to hear the difference between one ATR with flat frequency response from 30 Hz to 22 kHz and another with flat response from 60 Hz to 18 kHz.

One performance factor which relates particularly to sweetening deserves mention here. This is *track-to-track crosstalk*, both in the play mode and in the record mode. Crosstalk typically comes from the intermingling of signals from two physically adjacent tracks of the tape. In playback, the head for one track will pick up the magnetic fields off the tape tracks on either side as well as the track beneath it. During selective track recording, a head that is playing back adjacent to a head that is recording will pick up the signal from its recording neighbor.

Crosstalk is, of course, undesirable, but it becomes a special consideration when dealing with time code. Levels of crosstalk which may be acceptable between two audio tracks may not be acceptable between a time code track and an audio signal track. Since in most cases two audio tracks will finally get mixed together in some ratio, small amounts of crosstalk have negligible effects on the final product. The smallest time code bleed, however, can ruin a good sound track. The old-fashioned, simple solution to time code crosstalk was to record time code on a track at the edge of the tape and leave the adjacent track empty, a *guard band*.

This is effective but uses up two tracks rather than one. Most modern ATRs have minimized track-to-track crosstalk to a level that allows use of tracks adjacent to the code. The absolute amount of code bleed is a function of the characteristic crosstalk and the level at which the code is recorded. The minimum acceptable level for the code depends on the reproduction characteristics of the deck and the input requirements of the time code reader. It is difficult to determine the ultimate performance in this regard from specifications alone. The best evidence will come from others using a similar configuration. Some ATR manufacturers are directing significant attention to this problem and offer more specific information on this application. For example, in a product brochure on its Series-50 ATRs, TASCAM says, ". . . you don't have to waste a track to keep SMPTE from leaking into the program if you record it at − 7 VU to − 10 VU." The authors' experience has verified this claim.

Crosstalk in the record mode between a recording channel and an adjacent playback channel can cause two different problems, depending on the track usage. These are feedback in the mix and contamination of the time code playback. In the class of ATRs suitable for small-scale sweetening, this type of crosstalk remains a problem regardless of the model deck used and must be avoided in the postproduction processes. Solutions to this problem will be discussed further in Chapter 7.

Another issue in evaluating multitrack ATRs for use in sweetening is the *punch-in* and *punch-out* characteristics. In other words, exactly what goes down onto the tape at the instant that the ATR is punched in to record mode or punched out of record mode? The ideal is that at the exact moment of the punch, whether activated by operator buttons or the remote control of an editor or synchronizer, the audio on tape makes an instantaneous change from the previously recorded material to the new input material, and vice versa at punch-out. In reality, the transition may be delayed a small but occasionally noticeable amount from the desired point, may put a signal on the tape which results in an audible artifact in playback (a *snivit*), or may create a hole in the recording at the transition point.

In video editing, the cuts or transitions analogous to the audio punch-in are timed to occur during the vertical interval. The vertical blanking time allows the electronics to prepare for recording before the next field of picture begins, so that the image appears to make an instantaneous change to the new material. In audio recording there is no blanking time to mask the electronic switchover to record mode. If the simplest form of switch is executed, the punch-in is rapid but creates an audio artifact on the tape often described as a "pop." More sophisticated electronics can be employed to control the switchover and eliminate the pop, giving what is termed "silent punch-in" (or punch-out, since the same principle may be used on both ends of the recording). The most common method employs a gradual increase or decrease in the record bias current, rather than an abrupt switch on or off.

Most of the ATRs that would be considered for use in a small-scale sweetening system will have some provision for silent punch-in. The disadvantage of the more basic type of silent punch-in circuit is that the activation of the record function takes a measurable amount of time, perhaps as long as 100 milliseconds. Since during this switchover time the previous material is being erased and the new material is not yet being recorded, there is no valid audio signal. If there is active audio on the existing program and if there is active audio on the new material, at the edit or punch-in point an audible hole or gap will be heard. Occasionally, the silent punch-in (or punch-out) will create an audible artifact of its own, not a pop but a muted hiss or buzz which is a product of the incoming audio and the bias control circuit.

The other disadvantage of silent punch-in is in the time delay

Fig. 6-6. Gapless punch-in is a feature typically found on studio machines costing upwards of $25,000, such as this Ampex MM-1200 2″ 24-track ATR (courtesy Ampex Corporation).

from the signaled record start until actual recording begins. This is only a problem when performing very tight edits using a time code editor, as in editing dialog for a theatrical-style program. Using the same time code numbers as in the video edit, the audio edit may be delayed by several frames, upcutting a word or adding a snivit at the end. Moving up to the top-of-the-line studio ATRs, further electronic sophistication is employed to perform both silent and "gapless" or nearly gapless punch-in (Fig. 6-6). Digital audio recorders are capable of perfectly silent and gapless punch-in.

These details of punching in and out (i.e., how silent, how long is the gap) are not included in the usual collection of published specs on an ATR. They may be partially discernible from the more technical documentation, but can be most accurately assessed through experience.

One final issue about the choice of an ATR is compatibility. If your postproduction facility is full-service, depending on no outside services, this is not a concern. More likely, however, there are times when audio material will come from outside sources on tape, or you will need to carry a sound track to another facility for layback. In either of these cases, you need an ATR compatible with your associates—an ATR which will play the same size tape, with the same number of tracks, at the same speed. The 1/2" 8-track machines touted earlier for their price/performance advantage suffer the disadvantage that they are relatively new and are not found in many postproduction facilities. Choosing such a machine gives little opportunity for compatibility. The most common, industry-standard types of ATR are the 1/4" 2-track (rarely found with time code control), and the 1/2" 4-track. The 1/4" is good for bringing in source material such as narration or wild sound effects. The 1/2" 4-track is most useful for laybacks, since most full-scale video post houses have a time code controlled 1/2" 4-track.

These compatibility issues may be leading to the conclusion that you really need two ATRs, and in the long run you probably will. To start, however, opt for one 1/2" 4-track; although very limited in track capacity, it will give outside compatibility. The best answer to the ATR question, of course, depends on your specific applications, postproduction methods, and budget.

MIXING CONSOLES

Mixing consoles are the next area of concern in the audio sweetening bay. The tendency is to purchase a large console offering much more capability than is required for the process. When merging a video edit bay and sweetening bay (which will be discussed in Chapter 10), space is always at a premium and a large mixing console simply may not fit. Careful consideration must be given to the actual requirements for a mixing console, vis-a-vis the type of work that will be done in the sweetening facility. It is advisable to select a console with sufficient inputs and outputs (buses and auxiliary outputs) to match the other equipment complement, such as the multitrack machine. For example, it is advisable when using an 8-track ATR, to have a mixer with eight buses. The TASCAM M-512 is a 12-input, 8-bus console with two additional auxiliary outputs; it is economically priced and is well suited for these environments and applications (Fig. 6-7). But there are dozens of options available and the selection of a mixing console must rely on personal taste, because they all offer very competitive capabilities and specifications (Fig. 6-8).

Consideration also must be given to audio *patching* capability. Even though most popular mixing consoles have many switchable inputs and auxiliary outputs that give extensive internal signal routing capability, as you expand you'll find it easy to accumulate more audio sends and returns than the mixer has inputs and outputs. Consoles like the TASCAM M-512, with eight buses and two auxiliaries, will reach the limit with multiple multitrack machines, such as an 8-track, 1/2" 4-track, and a standard 1/4" 2-track ATR.

To solve this problem, TASCAM has introduced its model 520, which is a 20-input, 8-bus mixer with four auxiliary outputs, making it better suited to complex sweetening environments. The 520 was actually designed for use with a 16-track recorder. Each of its

Fig. 6-7. The TASCAM M-50 and its successor, the M-512, are both 12-input, 8-bus mixing consoles and are about the smallest and least expensive consoles suitable for 8-track environments (courtesy TASCAM).

Fig. 6-8. Yamaha also manufacturers a line of "low-end" consoles suitable for sweetening (courtesy Yamaha).

eight buses has two parallel outputs on the back panel for feeding two inputs of a 16-track. For example, buses 1 through 8 of the mixer can be connected to ATR inputs 1 through 8, respectively, and also connected to ATR inputs 9 through 16. In this configuration, the console has 16 input connections dedicated to ATR outputs. The arriving signals can be routed to an input channel or the monitor section independently.

In an 8-track environment, the other eight tape inputs can be used for auxiliary ATRs, such as a 4-track and a 2-track. Similarly, in an 8-track environment the second output from each bus could be used to send to the auxiliary 4-track and 2-track, subject to the constraint that simultaneous recording of *different* material to parallel devices, e.g., the 8-track and the 4-track, is impossible.

Other devices which must pass through the console are the phonograph, the audio cassette deck, and (of course) the VTRs. At a minimum the console must receive inputs from each of these devices and send an output to the record VTR. For general convenience it is desirable to have inputs and outputs to every device accessible through the console. The TASCAM 512 and 520, with switchable inputs and twin bus outputs, provide enough flexibility to handle an array of devices. Choosing the optimum configuration

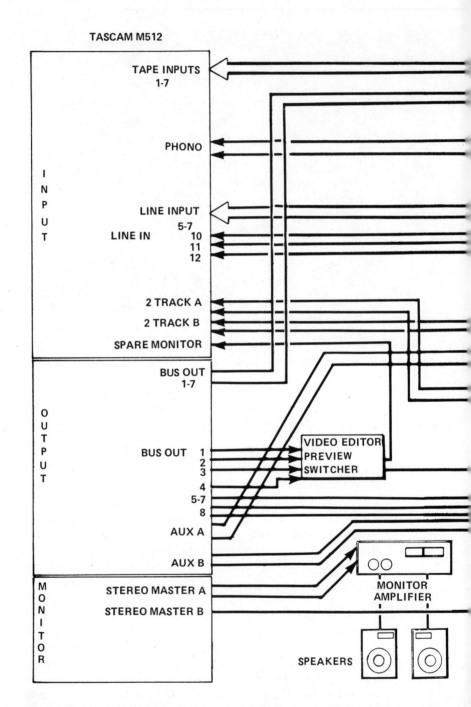

Fig. 6-9. The TASCAM M-512 console has versatile input, output, and internal routing capabilities. This is a sample wiring configuration for use in an integrated video editing and sweetening system.

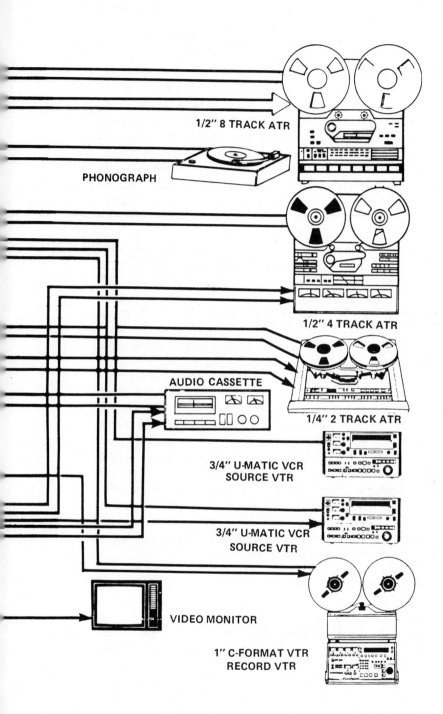

1/2" 8 TRACK ATR

PHONOGRAPH

1/2" 4 TRACK ATR

AUDIO CASSETTE

1/4" 2 TRACK ATR

3/4" U-MATIC VCR
SOURCE VTR

3/4" U-MATIC VCR
SOURCE VTR

VIDEO MONITOR

1" C-FORMAT VTR
RECORD VTR

depends on the available decks, the sweetening processes employed, and personal preference. One sample arrangement of inputs and outputs to a 512 is illustrated in Fig. 6-9.

With other consoles having fewer inputs and outputs or less internal routing ability, an external patch panel is the only solution. Similar to a video patch panel in a video edit bay, an audio patch panel is set up with normal connections for the most common uses of the limited inputs and outputs. The normal connections are made either internally in the panel or with bridging plugs or cords. Alternate signal routes are created by plugging patch cords into the panel. In sweetening, various machines exchange roles during various stages of the process. In the laydown, the record VTR is the source and the ATR is the record machine, while in layback the situation is reversed. A patch panel will greatly facilitate these routing changes. Figure 6-10 is a diagram of a system with a small mixer and patch panel. Professional-grade patch panels are built for three-wire balanced audio, with internal normal connections which are broken when a patch cord is inserted. A more economical solution for small-scale sweetening is a two-wire, unbalanced panel made with RCA connectors and no internal normal connections. A TASCAM patching panel is shown in Fig. 6-11.

The next element needed in the audio hardware chain is the monitor speaker and amplifier stage. You can't mix it if you can't hear it, and what you hear in your sweetening bay needs to resemble what will be heard by the intended audience. It is most desirable to have a very good pair of reference or monitor speakers (such as the JBL 4411 series) with a powerful stereo amplifier, in addition to a small speaker or TV speaker to represent how the mix will ultimately be heard (Figs. 6-12 and 6-13). Most mixing consoles can accommodate two separate outputs, one that can be directed to the high-quality "hear every imperfection" monitor speakers, and the other output directed to the "let's see what we can get away with" speaker.

Once the system is configured, it must be calibrated. This means that what goes in must equal what goes out. Calibration should be checked periodically, perhaps before each sweetening session. Most mixing consoles have test tone generators built in, and most also have trimming capability on the inputs. Simply put, this process consists of feeding a tone to the bus (any and all buses, one at a time) so that a 0 dB reading is indicated on both the mixing console and whatever track or channel of the device (ATR or VTR) that you intend to calibrate. When using a TASCAM M-50 console and Model 58 multitrack, switches on the rear of the console must be set to -10 dBV so that 0 dB on the console equals

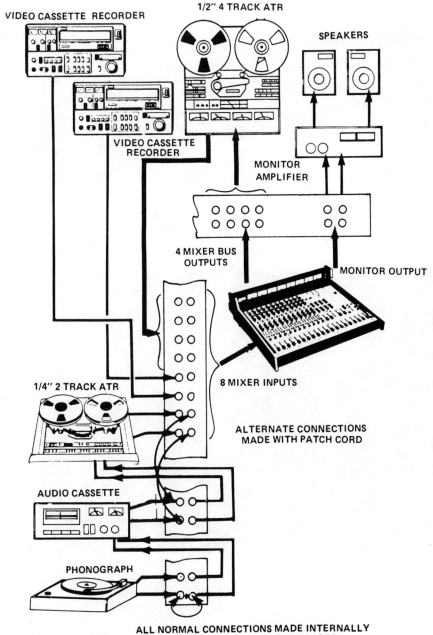

VIDEO CASSETTE RECORDER

1/2" 4 TRACK ATR

SPEAKERS

VIDEO CASSETTE RECORDER

MONITOR AMPLIFIER

4 MIXER BUS OUTPUTS

MONITOR OUTPUT

8 MIXER INPUTS

1/4" 2 TRACK ATR

ALTERNATE CONNECTIONS MADE WITH PATCH CORD

AUDIO CASSETTE

PHONOGRAPH

ALL NORMAL CONNECTIONS MADE INTERNALLY OR WITH BRIDGING PLUG OR PATCH CORD

Fig. 6-10. The audio patch panel provides convenient routing of audio signals between multiple audio devices and the mixing console.

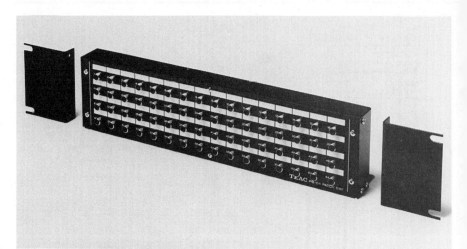

Fig. 6-11. The TASCAM RCA connector patch panel (courtesy TASCAM).

Fig. 6-12. Analogous to the video monitor, studio monitors such as the JBL 4401 are an essential reference for sweetening (courtesy JBL).

Fig. 6-13. Since mixing consoles have only line-level outputs, a power amplifier must be used to drive the monitor speakers (courtesy Yamaha).

0 dB on the multitrack. On equipment that has input level controls, such as the Otari 5050 series, adjust the input control to the 0 dB level. Next, record some tape with the test tone at 0 dB; a minute or so will suffice. Then rewind the tape to the beginning of the tones and play them back through the remix position (if calibrating the multitrack), or the appropriate input (in the case of a VTR or other machine). Set the pot or trimmer (marked RMX-Trim) so that a 0 dB indication is read on the appropriate meter. This calibration step will assure that signals leaving the console and coming back are equal.

The next patching element to be dealt with is time code. Time code is one of those "necessary evils." You need it, you need it to be clean, you don't want to contaminate any audio signal with it, but at the same time you need to have control over its volume in certain situations.

Time code must be recorded on both video tape and audio tape, either by prestriping (as in making both video and multitrack audio record masters), or by postcoding (as in coding field masters, music, or narration tracks). During the actual steps of the sweetening process, the time code is only played back and used for machine synchronization.

First of all, time code should be kept "clean" in that it shouldn't unnecessarily be run through too many line amplifier or amp stages because that deteriorates the square wave. When recording time code to a VTR or ATR, if you have input level controls on the recording machines (such as most VTRs and the Otari 5050 multitracks, but *not* the TASCAM 58), then it is best to run directly from the time code generator to the input channel. On the other hand, if you are recording time code to a TASCAM 58 or other machine which has no level control in the input, then the code first must be patched through a device that can control the level. Three such devices are immediately available: a VTR, an ATR, or a mixing console. The mixing console is the least desirable due to the number of amplifier stages involved in getting the signal in and out—unless you carefully follow the schematic diagram and find the most direct route. Additionally, it is best to patch the time code through the console only temporarily when striping tapes; it isn't good to mix time code with regular audio sources. The bottom line, however, is that most consoles utilizing 1980s technology have little leakage, and the amp stages don't tear up the time code too much.

OUTBOARD EQUIPMENT

As in a recording studio, outboard audio processing equipment is sometimes necessary and frequently desirable in an audio sweetening bay. Outboard equipment includes noise reduction (dbx and Dolby), compressor/limiters, companders, noise gates, echo and reverb, etc.

Using dbx or Dolby noise reduction equipment helps eliminate picking up the additional noise inherent in going through multiple tape generations, as happens during the sweetening process. The first generational loss is incurred during laydown (this is the second generational loss when the audio tracks are being taken from the EM). The third generational loss is incurred during the mix, and the fourth generational loss is incurred when you lay back to the EM. Dolby or dbx noise reduction in the process will minimize picking up noise during these generations (Fig. 6-14).

The most important rule for using noise reduction is that it must be encoded and decoded each time the signal is played back or recorded. You cannot record an encoded signal without experiencing some decay in the signal due to calibration. Thus, if you encode the signal prior to recording it on the multitrack (during the track-building process, for example), then you must also decode and reencode the signal during the mixing session, so that ultimately seven changes of noise reduction are required. Another important rule is that you cannot mix and match the different types of noise reduction, meaning that if your material was *encoded* with Dolby B, then it must be *decoded* with Dolby B, and so on. If you have such noise reduction equipment available, it should be used between other source machines and the multitrack ATR during track-building as well, being careful to encode and decode properly.

A most useful device in the sweetening process is the *compressor/limiter* (Fig. 6-15). A trade publication advertisement several years ago had a headline which read, "How to put a ten-pound load ·in a five-pound bag," which describes well the function of the device. Use compressor/limiters when the dynamic range of the source material, in terms of volume, goes beyond what you can effectively set the pot to reach as a happy medium. Let the needle bounce around enough to get good volume, keeping things up out of the noise, but don't let the volume go high enough to distort. One of the most essential uses for a compressor/limiter is in building tracks of narration or dialog or, more often, interviewing people who speak with a wide dynamic range. You can't possibly ride a pot fast enough to keep the needle centered when the person normally speaks softly but raises the volume of speech when excited.

The meter on a compressor/limiter operates "in reverse" compared to a standard VU or dB meter, in that the needle moves from right to left when it is compressing a loud passage—just the opposite of the VU meter monitoring the source. Care must be taken when using a compressor/limiter not to overcompress, which will make the signal sound like it is being "squished."

Although most mixing consoles have equalization capability for each channel, it may be desirable to obtain additional capability that can be patched in and out of other channels at will, as different situations demand. Outboard equalization is available in several types, including parametric and graphic equalizers. Parametric equalization resembles the capability available in most consoles, offering the ability to add or subtract volume (or dB) at given frequencies. The most widely accepted definition of a parametric equalizer is a device that provides continuously variable control over

Fig. 6-14. The dbx noise reduction system is a very useful piece of outboard equipment, especially for sweetening, because of the number of generations many elements go through during the process (courtesy TASCAM).

Fig. 6-15. A compressor/limiter is used when the dynamic range of a voice, instrument, or sound effect is too great to effectively control with movement of the fader on the console (courtesy Orban Associates, Inc.).

the three basic parameters of EQ: the amount of boost or dip in volume (dB); the frequency at which that boost or dip occurs; and the bandwidth or "Q," the amount by which frequencies on either side of the selected frequency are affected by the boost or dip.

Graphic equalizers offer the ability to dip or boost volume at specific frequencies, usually in octave increments. Graphic equalizers probably got their name from the visual reference obtained by the appearance of the controls, side-by-side slide pots which graphically represent the equalization that is occurring. If you wanted to boost the high and low end but dip (or "roll off") the midrange, the controls on a graphic equalizer would look like those in Fig. 6-16.

Outboard equalization is especially good for eliminating the noise level above 12 kHz, which is inherent in the 3/4" video cassette format and is amplified by the generational loss incurred during laydown and track building. Rolling it off with a graphic equalizer or "notching" it out with a parametric equalizer (Fig. 6-17) can help to reduce the hiss dramatically. Noise, rumble, or other

Fig. 6-16. A graphic equalizer shows "graphically" how the signal is being shaped (courtesy Orban Associates, Inc.).

100

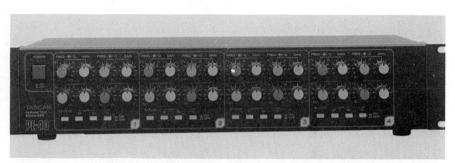

Fig. 6-17. This 4-channel parametric equalizer offers much more capability than is available through equalization in most low-cost consoles. This particular equalizer, offered by TASCAM, also has high- and low-pass filters on each channel (courtesy TASCAM).

audio garbage that was recorded in the field on the master tapes, such as from air conditioner blowers, traffic, or other extraneous sounds, can be equalized out of the track much more easily with an outboard parametric equalizer than by using what is available with the internal EQ capability of most low-cost mixing consoles. *Notch filters* are really fixed parametric equalizers that are set up to take a very specific frequency "notch" out of a track.

High-pass and low-pass filtering can also be accomplished with parametric or graphic equalizers so no sound above or below a given frequency will be allowed through the equalizer. High-pass filtering rolls off all sound below a certain frequency and can be tuned to frequencies between 20 and 200 Hz, while low-pass filtering lets low frequency sounds through and is selectable from 2 kHz to 20 kHz. Many outboard filter systems are available (Fig. 6-18).

Other useful outboard equipment in the audio sweetening bay are digital delay and digital reverb systems, aural exciters, noise gates, and multifunctional devices such as compellors. Although this equipment is often seen in high-end recording studios and

Fig. 6-18. The "565" filter set manufactured by JBL/UREI is a combination high- and low-pass filter, plus a notch and peak filter (courtesy JBL).

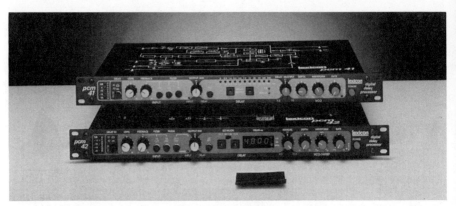

Fig. 6-19. Digital delay systems, such as these devices manufactured by Lexicon, offer the capability of "thickening" a sound or doing other special effects (courtesy Lexicon, Inc.).

Hollywood-scale sweetening bays, most small-scale budgets would run out well before being able to install these devices.

One use for digital delay during the sweetening process is to "thicken" a sound, in much the same way "slap-echo" (from the third head of an additional ATR, for example) will make a voice or effect sound much bigger and fuller (Fig. 6-19). Another application for digital delay is to make reverberation sound bigger without letting it get muddy. For instance, you can make a room sound like a bigger room by delaying the send, placing the digital delay ahead of the reverb device. You can also use digital delay for creating sound effects and making them sound bigger. Thickening them in stereo, delaying one part of the effect to the other channel, can make an effect such as a door slam appear bigger. Using digital delay in this form can give a voice or sound effect two dimensions instead of one.

Digital reverb is more natural-sounding than plate or spring systems and can be put in the same room as the monitor speakers

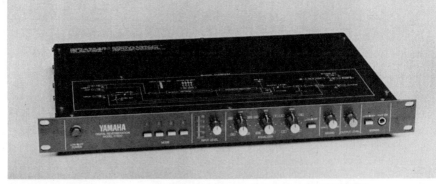

Fig. 6-20. A two-channel, spring-type reverberation unit (courtesy TASCAM).

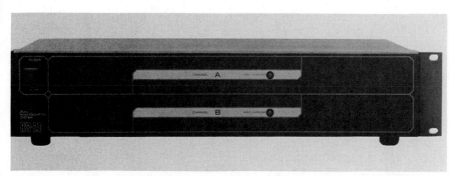

Fig. 6-21. A digital reverberation system manufactured by Yamaha (courtesy Yamaha).

without having to worry about feedback, while EMT plates take up lots of space and will cause feedback if placed near the monitor speakers (Figs. 6-20 and 6-21). You can use reverb to give a narrator some separation from other dialog, to create a particular ambience, and to make sounds more lifelike. When using reverb with music, you might require a delay of 2 or 3 seconds to achieve the desired ambience. When sweetening, however, a delay of 0.7 to 1.5 seconds to create ambience will suffice. A good rule of thumb is that short reverb gives ambience without destroying presence.

Aural exciters were designed to give back the transients and dynamics that are lost during the recording process, such as the loss of high frequencies from repeated use of tape. The aural exciter replaces upper harmonics, enhances voices, and gives more natural presence without changing voice color, as can happen with equalization. An aural exciter adds back the natural brightness, or presence, that is lost during the recording process, and it can be tuned to achieve a desired effect.

Another useful device is a noise gate, which can help keep tracks clean by turning off background noise when there is no other signal present. The noise gate has a trigger that can be set; when the audio signal exceeds that trigger threshold, the gate opens and lets the signal through. The release time can also be set so that the gate will not turn off until a predetermined amount of time has elapsed. If you have several talents on different tracks, each track having its own presence, then that presence noise is additive. Noise gates can cut out such noise, but you might have to replace the presence with a presence loop if no one is talking and the noise gates on each channel have canceled the presence.

One final device is the *compellor*, a multifunctional unit that combines the functions of compression, peak limiting, and leveling, and may have other features including noise-gating and stereo enhancement.

Chapter 7

System Configuration
and Operation

con • fig • u • ra • tion \ kən-fig-(y)ə - ′ra-shən \ *n*
the arrangement and linkage of sweetening hardware components

One of the oft-repeated premises of this book is that new technology
has yielded low-cost equipment that makes audio sweetening cost-
effective for small-scale video productions. Despite this fact, it is
a rare video producer who can commit to audio sweetening and
immediately purchase and install a complete, stand-alone sweetening facility. More representative of the small-scale environment is
the case where the producer commits to audio sweetening but must
acquire the hardware over time, as funds allow. At each step of
the upgrade, the new gear must be integrated with the existing
postproduction system and must provide some level of increased
productivity. Most likely, the small-scale video producer will never
need a full-function sweetening system, but would be better served
by having some sweetening capabilities integrated with his video
editing system. The audio producer who wants to expand his services, on the other hand, will want to utilize all his audio power.
He too needs to integrate a sweetening system with existing
facilities, and perhaps he too must do so in a phased installation
program.

To address the issue of integration of sweetening into video or audio production systems, several cases must be distinguished, since the implementation of sweetening will vary depending on the equipment, applications, and production methods already in place. This discussion will begin with the most basic configuration, the one where no equipment is already in place; call this the "From Scratch" case. The second case will be integrating sweetening into a control track video editing system, followed by a time code editing case. Configurations using synchronizer controllers and synchronizers with external computer control are the final two topics of this chapter.

As in the chapter on basic hardware, the emphasis here is on the synchronization and control aspects of the systems, for this problem is unique to sweetening. Integration of new equipment from an audio standpoint is a classic audio problem and is touched upon elsewhere.

Sweetening systems increase in complexity in two dimensions. In the audio dimension, higher-power systems have more audio machines, more audio tracks, and more audio processing equipment. In the control dimension, more sophisticated systems have more electronic control over the execution of the sweetening operations.

In an ideal system, all of the audio and video tape decks would be controlled through a single control console. The operator could directly actuate any machine individually, synchronize machines in pairs or combinations, execute edits as with video editors, maintain edit lists, and so on. There are systems that will do all these things and more, but they could not be considered "entry level" for the small-scale producer. Many of the high-powered video tape edit controllers are capable of anchoring such a sweetening system. Equipped with interfaces for both video and audio tape decks, edit controllers like the CMX 340 or the ISC models provide highly integrated, versatile control for a sweetening system. Many Hollywood sweetening houses are built around these types of video editors. The newest generation of intelligent synchronizer controllers, e.g., the Cipher Digital Softouch and the Adams-Smith Event/Edit Controller, are also providing this integrated control capability, even including edit lists.

Short of a totally integrated editing/ sweetening controller, what subset of the ideal machine control functions may be achievable in a small-scale system? First and already understood is primitive synchronization of video and multitrack audio; this is the minimum for sweetening on any scale. Next is *automatic record trigger*, the ability to punch in and out of record mode accurately and repeatably at time code cues. This affords precise editing for time-critical effects. With these two functions almost any sweetening can be performed . . . somehow. From here on, enhanced control features add to convenience and efficiency more than to functionality. The list continues to include direct machine control of the decks, automatic cuing, multiple machine cue/roll/record sequences for edits, and then on into edit lists, ADR looping, etc.

In building a small-scale sweetening system these sophisticated controls will not be available, so alternative methods to get the job done must be considered while planning the system.

FROM SCRATCH

The most basic configuration begins with no video postproduction at all. Consider a hypothetical producer who edits outside, usually on a U-matic, control track, cuts-only system. From time to time he does a project which he edits at the local TV station, with time code, from 3/4" to 1". He has one VTR (let's say a Sony 5850) and he's ready to embark on some basic sweetening. The audio producer entering sweetening is in a similar position, except that he must first buy a VTR.

To get rolling, he must start with a multitrack audio tape recorder. A 1/2" 4-track like an Otari MX5050 or a TASCAM 44 might be his first choice. An 8-track would be more versatile but may not be in the budget right now. The next required item is a mixing console, one with at least eight inputs and four outputs, or maybe more for the sake of future expansion. Many choices are available from TASCAM, Yamaha, Soundcraft and others.

A basic synchronizer with one machine interface for the ATR will be his starter controller. Having chosen one of the modern, popular model ATRs, every synchronizer will have an interface available for his deck—Cipher Digital, Adams-Smith, Audio Kinetics, Sony, you name it. Let's say he buys an Adams-Smith System 2600 with three modules, power supply, transport controller, and longitudinal time code reader.

One more hardware unit, a time code generator, is not mandatory because the video material and the audio tapes could be time coded at another facility, but having the generator on hand would save much time and trouble. Time code generators are available from any number of sources; EECO, Gray Engineering, and ESE are a few, but a convenient alternative in this case would be to add a time code generator module into the Adams-Smith unit.

Adding to these major items an audio cassette player, a phonograph, and an amplifier with a monitor speaker rounds out the system. Figure 7-1 shows the connection of the units. A 1/4" audio tape deck is included, since it is most useful for bringing in

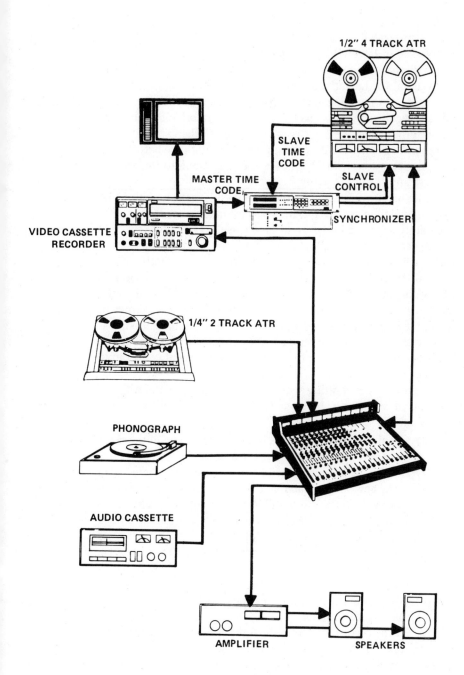

Fig. 7-1. Basic stand-alone sweetening. This system operates independently of the video editing process.

audio material from outside studios (narration, music, and sound effects, for example) but could be sacrificed by using audio cassettes at the cost of lowered audio quality.

With this minimum system our hypothetical producer is ready to sweeten. Of the automatic machine control functions proposed for the ideal sweetening system, this one has only synchronization; all else becomes the responsibility of the operator. When the synchronizer is active, the ATR is slaved to the VTR and the operator controls the motion of both through the VTR. With the buttons and shuttle dial on the 5850, he moves the video tape to the area of interest and the ATR follows.

One of the modules in the specified synchronizer is the longitudinal time code (LTC) reader. This module reads time code accurately over a wide range of tape speeds, typically from 1/20 play speed to 100 times play speed. In the present case, this allows the synchronizer to follow the master video tape in shuttle mode. Without the LTC reader, the synchronizer could read code and follow only at speeds near play speed and would get lost when the master went into high-speed shuttle. As discussed in Chapter 5, use of the high-speed reader will necessitate a wideband modification for the 5850 VTR. Even in a low-budget starter system, this module is recommended for the resultant improvement in operating efficiency.

In the typical operating sequence for recording to the ATR either in laydown or track building, the operator executes the following scenario.

1) Cue the VTR to a point in the program ahead of the point of record start, with the ATR following.
2) Cue the audio source device to a point an equal time ahead of the new source material. For laydown of the edited audio from video cassette to ATR, this is not necessary.
3) Establish the proper routing of the audio from the source to the proper track of the ATR.
4) Enable the record function for that ATR track.
5) Simultaneously start the source device and the VTR in play mode, while the ATR follows.
6) Watch that the synchronizer achieves lock prior to the actual record in point.
7) At the record in point, punch the ATR into record mode.
8) At the record out point, punch the ATR out of record.

These are only the mechanical operations that follow the creative processes of selection, leveling, EQ, etc., and they become automatic with time. The point is that the operator has much responsibility in this level of system. While the synchronizer is a necessary tool for laydown, layback, and for viewing the picture during building and mixing, most of the control functions are left to the operator.

Still, this system is capable of producing rather sophisticated sound tracks. The greatest difficulty will be found in building tracks with tightly synchronized sound. This includes dialog from on-camera talent and precise effects (a door slam, for example), where the effect must coincide precisely with the visual.

On-camera dialog tracks would be extremely difficult to build in the sweetening process, so the first operating rule in this environment is that all on-camera dialog must be edited into the audio track during the video edit. This track from the video edit master is laid down to one track on the ATR. Music with visuals cut to the beat must be treated similarly or else the operator must deal with the trial-and-error process of trying to repeat sync in the post-edit sweetening session.

Laying tightly synchronized sound effects to precisely align with picture will be difficult, whether the effect comes from the original video cassette or from an effects record. Exact timing of effects from non-sync sources 1/4″, audio cassette, or phono can only be achieved by trial and error. From video cassette, the synchronizer with its offset function can be used to lay in the effect precisely, but the complicating factor is that the program picture is not available when laying the effect because the VTR is being used for the audio source. The clever operator learns techniques and devises solutions to these problems.

The manual punch-in and punch-out can be a constraint if bunched effects are being built onto a single ATR track. The operator must be very accurate with his punch-in fingers in order to preserve the previously recorded effects. Otherwise he must resort to using multiple tracks and a submix for the grouped effects.

One thing is certain: Working with a system like this can create a very fundamental understanding of what the more sophisticated controllers are doing and an appreciation for the extra capabilities and efficiencies they provide. The synchronizer is a very versatile device and allows many alternatives for upgrading. If the producer leans toward more involvement with video editing, the synchronizer may be integrated with a video editor. If he decides to expand sweetening without video editing, additional synchronizers and a synchronizer controller may be his choice.

CONTROL TRACK EDITING

The next case study is a producer with a control track editing system. He also has basic audio equipment, a 1/4″ audio deck, an audio cassette and phonograph with a 4 × 2 mixer. He currently does limited sweetening by hot-rolling the music or effects and ping-ponging between the two channels of his VTR. By the time he has three layers of audio, the tape hiss is almost unacceptable. He wants better audio quality and the ability to incorporate synchronized natural sound beds from the field master video tape.

Although starting from a different position, this producer can start into sweetening with much the same new hardware as the previous example. Integrating with the video editor, his system configuration will be slightly more complex and his operation methods will combine some of the sweetening processes with the video editing to take full advantage of the increased capability of the integrated system.

The system is illustrated in Fig. 7-2 with a 4-track ATR and an 8 × 4 mixer as in the first sample case, but this producer may well wish he had eight tracks and a matched board as he develops his techniques.

Extracting the machine control portion from the entire system, Fig. 7-3 reaffirms that this is essentially a two-machine editing system with an ATR tagging along behind the record VTR. Simplifying even further, think of the combined VTR and ATR as a single unit, a VTR with multiple audio tracks. As such, the system reduces to a simple two-machine system. It is helpful to keep this simplification in mind when conceptualizing solutions to operational puzzles. This analogy falls short in one functional aspect: The editing system will not trigger the record function of the ATR as it does the VTR. When previewing or recording a video edit, with the ATR following the record VTR, audio may be recorded onto the ATR by manually activating the record function while the machines are rolling in sync. The audio will thus be recorded on the 4-track audio tape in the exact position matching the video on the edit master cassette.

The ability to record to the ATR during the video edit session enhances the functionality and efficiency of sweetening. This capability is especially useful when dealing with synchronized sound. With the system in the preceding example, lacking an edit controller, the only reliable way to guarantee sync when synchronized sound was required was to record during the video edit session onto the audio channel of the video tape, at the exclusion of any other audio for that program time period. With the present configuration, however, such a constraint does not exist.

Consider the case where a narrator is speaking over live footage with essential natural sound. The narrator is the pacing element and must be recorded first in order to cut the visuals. When

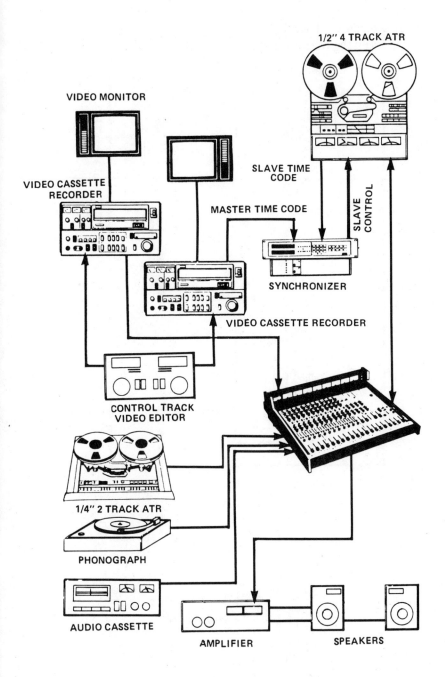

1/2" 4 TRACK ATR

VIDEO MONITOR

VIDEO CASSETTE
RECORDER

SLAVE TIME
CODE

MASTER TIME CODE

SLAVE
CONTROL

SYNCHRONIZER

VIDEO CASSETTE RECORDER

CONTROL TRACK
VIDEO EDITOR

1/4" 2 TRACK ATR

PHONOGRAPH

AUDIO CASSETTE

AMPLIFIER   SPEAKERS

Fig. 7-2. A complete basic sweetening system integrated with a control track video editing system.

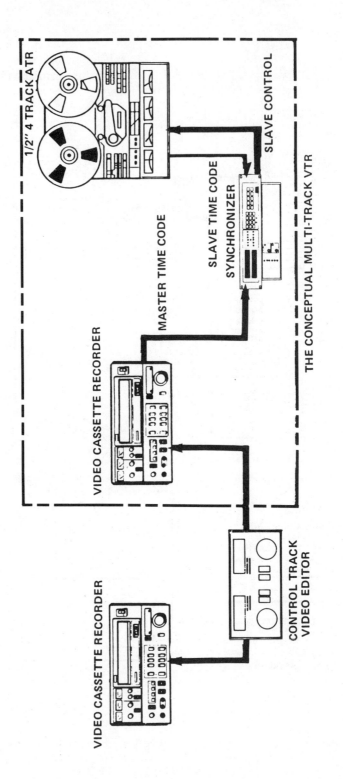

Fig. 7-3. The control and synchronization portion of the basic control track sweetening system.

recording the visuals, the natural sound can be routed to the ATR; by punching in at the video edit point, the natural sound will be recorded in sync with video. Remember that the natural sound must be recorded during the edit of the matched video, because exact sync would be difficult to duplicate in postedit sweetening without time code accuracy. For optimal audio quality, the narrator also might also be recorded directly to an open track on the ATR, rather than to the video cassette. Except for the manual punch-in and punch-out, this is no more difficult operationally.

Following this principle, it is clear how other types of synchronized sound may be recorded directly to the ATR during the video edit. Dialog with overlapping lines is a good example. Another situation prompting direct recording to the ATR is one where visuals will be cut to the beat of a music cue. The music must be recorded before editing the visuals, so duplicating sync in post sweetening would be difficult. The music cue could be recorded on the video cassette prior to cutting the visuals, but then the cue would have to be transferred to the ATR for the mix. The music would go through another generation, that generation being video cassette.

The guiding principles here are that recording to the ATR during the video edit is recommended for any audio where it would be difficult to reproduce the sync with video later on. Secondarily, anything recorded directly to the ATR will have better audio quality in the final product.

Using the ATR as part of the editing system facilitates another track-building function that was difficult with the most basic system: recording tight sound effects. Sound effects from libraries on records or 1/4″ tape can be transferred to video cassette and then edited into position on the ATR similar to sound from the field masters. Once again this makes use of the video editor to mark, cue, and sync the source material relative to the program, while the operator must route the signal and punch in and out on the ATR. This method does incur an additional generation between source and final program track, but typically for sound effects this concern is negligible compared to the production efficiency.

Comparing the automatic functions of this system with those of the potential functions of the ideal system, this system has the mandatory synchronization and a limited form of machine-to-machine editing, but is limited by the lack of automatic punch-in and by control track accuracy. The lack of automatic record trigger is really only a constraint for audio edits requiring precise in and out points. Control track editing demands that some track building be done during rather than after the video edit.

When the video edit is complete, the remainder of the sweetening may proceed per the standard format. The audio track edited to an audio channel of the record VTR may be laid down to the ATR. Then the remainder of the track-building continues, hot-rolling material in from the non-sync devices, 1/4", audio cassette, and phono, and editing from the source VTR. By leaving the ATR slaved to the VTR through the synchronizer and manipulating the system through the editor or the VTR itself, the video picture is always available through each stage of the process, laydown, track building, mixing, and layback.

On the subject of punch-in and punch-out on the ATR, many synchronizers have the ability to trigger external devices or events with logic or contact closure outputs; these may be programmed to activate on master time code cues. The basic synchronizer specified in these early examples may not have the means for entering such a request without purchasing an additional console module. Even if this function can be accessed, in a control track editing environment the time code of the edit in-point is not readily available, and on top of that the extra effort to enter it into the synchronizer would be justified only by an occasional critical edit.

If a bit of custom electronic work were within the capabilities of a producer using a control track editing system, a handy feature for this system would be an electronic punch-in and punch-out controlled by the editor for the ATR. Access to the record trigger signal lines into the ATR is usually quite straightforward through the remote control connector. Extracting the record signal that normally goes to the VTR from the editor may be more difficult; if it can be identified, however, a simple electrical black box might be designed to provide the extra convenience and accuracy of timed, electronic punch-in.

Another home-brew feature which might be added to this type of system is a play trigger for the non-sync devices. Tapping into the interface from the editor to either the source or the record VTR, the play mode activation signal could be used to start a 1/4" ATR or a cassette deck. The advantage of such an auto-start comes when recording material from a non-sync source, aligned with particular visual action. This is often a trial-and-error process, but the auto-start eliminates some of the uncertainty in the sync attempts and leaves the cuing position as the single variable for adjusting the material placement in the program.

This class of system, control track editor with synchronizer, is quite capable of producing sophisticated multilayer audio. Its main deficiency, lack of time code editing accuracy, will occasionally constrain either the program character or production efficiency.

TIME CODE EDITING

The next postproduction environment is denoted by time code editing; two, three, or more VTRs controlled with a time code editor with or without edit list capabilities. The hypothetical producer (or production company, as might be more representative in this case) wanting to expand into sweetening first faces a fundamental choice between two control configurations: direct interface from the editor to the ATR or auxiliary synchronization.

For some this will not be an issue since not all time code editing systems offer interfaces to ATRs; as such, the only choice is to use a synchronizer. On the other hand, if the editing system has the option of interfaces to ATRs, there are a number of factors to be analyzed in choosing whether to use that interface or to use an external synchronizer. Among the factors to consider are the number of decks allowed simultaneously on line, the definition of the record machine, the ability for multiple machine rolls and records, edit list features, and of course, cost.

The two types of system configuration are diagrammed in Figs. 7-4 and 7-5, but the significant differences appear in the operations of the systems. With the external synchronizer, operating methods are very similar to the previous example with the control track editor. Having time code, however, facilitates some functions that are not possible or are very difficult with the control track system. In principle, time code accuracy allows perfect repetition of record events, so absolutely synchronized sound may be recorded simultaneously with the video edit or in a postedit sweetening session. Otherwise, operation in this environment is very similar to the previous scenario. Recall the analogy of the multitrack VTR. Edits are constructed from the source machines to the locked VTR-ATR pair; the two always roll together, giving synchronized picture and sound.

With the direct interface to the ATR, the program picture and sound are not always locked together. The two decks are treated separately by the editor. To maintain locked audio and video, edits must be constructed to ensure that both machines play together at matched time code. For example, the system can be configured such that one VTR is the record machine, while two VTRs and the ATR are source machines. A master shot's video and audio have been recorded to the VTR and ATR, respectively. A video-only insert shot must now be placed within the master shot based on an audio cue. To roll the record VTR, the ATR in sync, and the source VTR for the insert, the editor will be programmed for a dissolve, giving the record VTR and the ATR identical in and out points. Similar manipulation of the editor must be done for

115

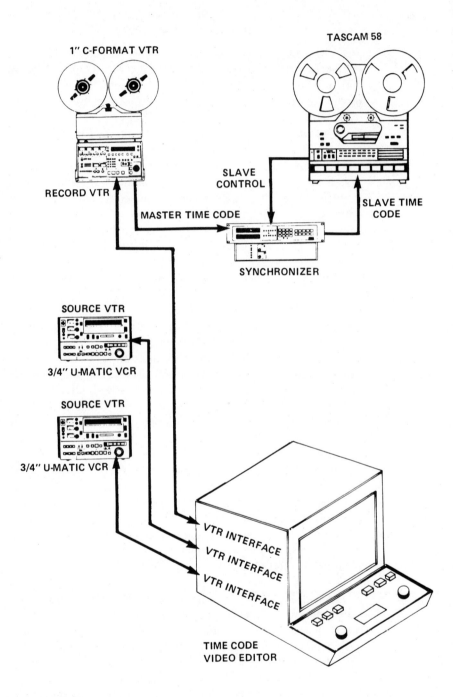

Fig. 7-4. Time code video editing system with integrated sweetening; here the ATR is controlled with the synchronizer.

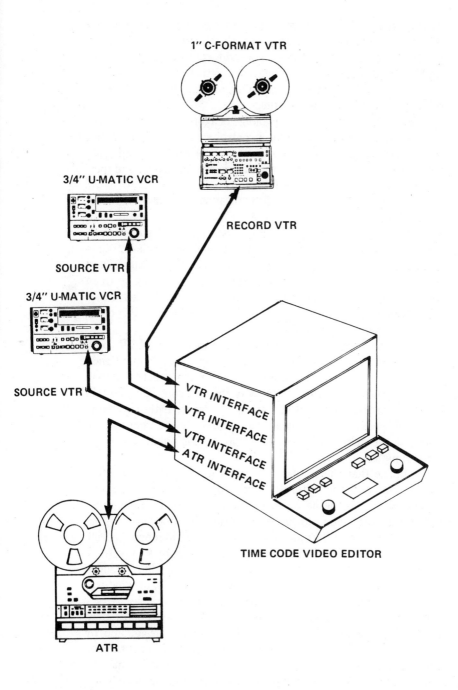

1" C-FORMAT VTR

3/4" U-MATIC VCR

RECORD VTR

SOURCE VTR

3/4" U-MATIC VCR

SOURCE VTR

VTR INTERFACE
VTR INTERFACE
VTR INTERFACE
ATR INTERFACE

TIME CODE VIDEO EDITOR

ATR

Fig. 7-5. Time code video editing system with integrated sweetening; in this version the ATR is controlled via a direct interface to the video editor.

117

various types of operations through the sweetening process. While this is representative of operations with the lower-end editors, it is not the case with all time code edit controllers. The more sophisticated machines have built-in functions to facilitate synchronous rolling of multiple machines or even special software packages for sweetening functions.

The greatest operational advantage of a direct interface system at any level is that the operator's control actions are unified and minimized because all machines are actuated through a single console, all events are constructed with similar edit dialog, and (perhaps) an edit list is available for all events.

Nominally, using external synchronization does not provide record punch-in and punch-out for the ATR or start signals for non-sync audio devices, but many time code editors have general-purpose logic or relay outputs available for such applications. While these programmable event triggers can be used to roll decks and to punch in or out, they require an extra measure of dialog between the operator and the edit controller. Still, this makes the task easier than trying to press buttons on three different machines at specific time code cues.

The time code system with direct interface to the ATR could be the foundation of the ideal control environment mentioned earlier, or it could be a very limited and awkward sweetening tool. The difference lies in the flexibility of the edit controller, both in hardware architecture and in software features. If the system is not flexible enough, an external synchronizer may be a better solution than the direct interface. To illustrate this point, consider a few examples.

Suppose that the project at hand requires A/B roll editing throughout, and the natural sound from video tape must be preserved behind the narrator. It would be most efficient to record the natural sound to the ATR during the video edit, as opposed to completing the video edit and returning to rebuild a track of the natural audio. However, the editor supports only three machines at a time. To record the natural sound during the video edit would mean unplugging cables, interface cards, or whatever between each edit—hardly an efficient solution.

Or, in the same situation, the edit controller may support more than three machines but the record machine is designated by physical connection rather than software. The ATR must then be connected as a source machine; while the natural sound may be recorded to the ATR, it requires manual punch-in and punch-out, which is no better than the externally synchronized configuration.

If the edit controller supports more than three source machines and allows the record machine to be designated through a console command, the audio edit of the natural sound to the ATR can be completed immediately following the video edit—simple, clean, efficient.

Elaborating further on this same example points out the influence of edit lists on the configuration decision. Speaking in favor of the directly interfaced ATR, if the natural sound must be recorded in postedit sweetening and the editor has produced an edit list, building the track of the natural sound becomes a routine autoassembly from the source video cassettes to the ATR as the record machine. This same technique may be used for on-camera dialog or narration where it is desirable to save a generation for the sake of absolute audio quality. The audio cut to the video master is thus like an off-line audio edit, and all the audio is rebuilt from the edit list.

One point regarding a time code system used principally for off-line work might be of interest. Adding sweetening capability to a time code system nominally used for off-line is a smart way to realize considerable savings at the out-of-house on-line session. Complete audio tracks built to the time code of the edit list on the in-house sweetening system can be carried into the on-line session on coded compatible media, such as 1/2" 4-track. In the on-line session, one audio edit is required to lay back the complete track.

Another issue related to the question of direct interface versus synchronizer is the plan for the future. What other synchronized sound source machines are possible acquisitions? A larger multitrack? Different format source VTRs? Does the edit controller have interfaces for these decks? Will it support enough machines simultaneously? The same might be asked of the candidate synchronizers. Generally, the synchronizers offer a wider variety of interface for audio machines than video editors do, and their architecture allows for greater expansion either internally or through ganged units. An expanded system may be planned with a mix of both types of control interface, using the advantages of each.

Finally, cost may be a significant factor. A basic synchronizer would be in the realm of $5000, while an interface to an editor would more likely be less than $2000. To many a small-scale producer, the difference may be significant.

A single conclusion to this discussion regarding direct editor interface versus synchronizer is deliberately missing. Too many factors enter the equation to allow a "recommended" system configuration. The best course of action is to study the options and try to envision the processes required for the types of production anticipated.

SYNCHRONIZER CONTROLLERS

Another approach to sweetening control systems is the use of synchronizers with dedicated synchronizer controllers. This type of configuration represents a larger investment in sweetening than has been considered in previous sections, but it offers versatile functionality in either an independent situation or integrated with a video editor.

Figure 7-6 illustrates a system that includes several machines with synchronizers and a synchronizer controller. Note that additional synchronizer modules are added for the additional controlled machines. The controller module houses the higher-level intelligence to accept commands from the operator and coordinate the actions of the distinct synchronizer modules. With the array of functions incorporated in the newest models, these controllers exhibit most of the characteristics of the ideal controller (at least in the independent sweetening environment) and could only be bested in combined video and sweetening by the high-powered video edit controllers. When designing a system for sweetening only, such a controller is the natural first choice; for the small-scale video producer who is growing into sweetening in phases, the synchronizer controller becomes a logical future upgrade.

Consider the sample cases discussed above and suppose that each respective producer has realized the value of sweetening and is prepared to add an 8-track ATR, planning to use the 8-track as the master ATR, and assigning the 4-track as a synchronized source for editing in narration and music and for transporting final tracks out for layback. Each could get by using only the basic synchronizer and constantly reconfiguring for the operation required. To improve the efficiency, the next upgrade would be to add automated control for both ATRs. Each could accomplish this with a synchronizer controller unit.

The producer without a video editor would configure his system as shown in Fig. 7-7 for laydown and for building from source materials on video cassette. For building tracks from ATR to ATR he would reconfigure to match Fig. 7-8. This second configuration would also serve for laying back or mixing to the 4-track if the final audio were to be transported out of house to a video mastering facility. The need for reconfiguration is inherent in these hybrid configurations; it can be relieved only by separating out sweetening from video editing and buying more synchronizing equipment, or by investing in a high-power, high-cost integrated control system.

If this producer desired to partially alleviate the reconfiguration hassles, he could add an additional synchronizer module and keep all three machines controlled and synchronized simul-

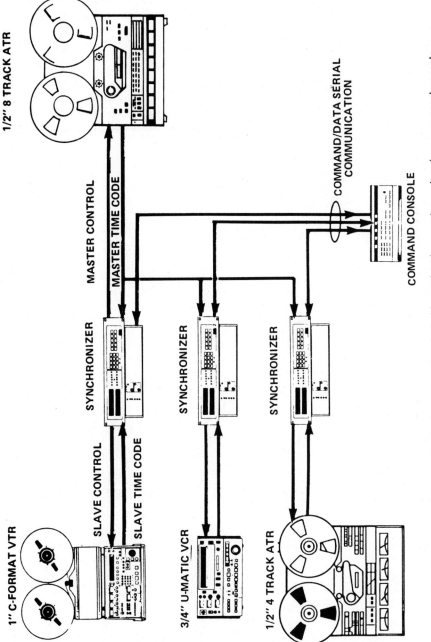

Fig. 7-6. A combination of several video and audio machines controlled with synchronizers and synchronizer command console.

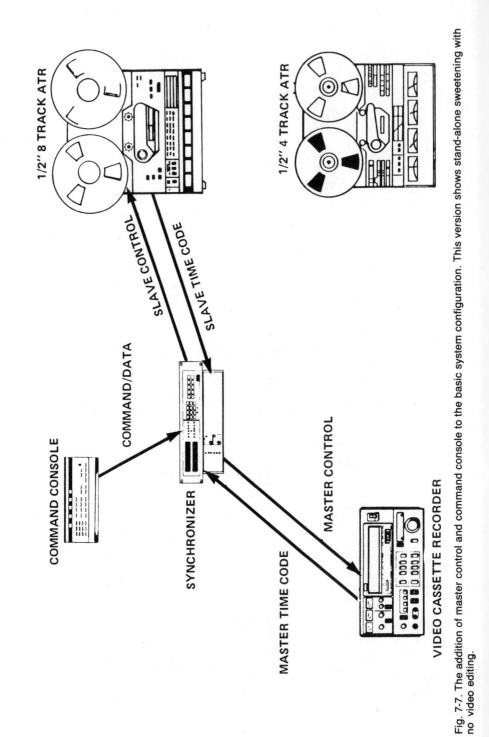

COMMAND CONSOLE

COMMAND/DATA

SYNCHRONIZER

1/2" 8 TRACK ATR

SLAVE CONTROL

SLAVE TIME CODE

1/2" 4 TRACK ATR

MASTER CONTROL

MASTER TIME CODE

VIDEO CASSETTE RECORDER

Fig. 7-7. The addition of master control and command console to the basic system configuration. This version shows stand-alone sweetening with no video editing.

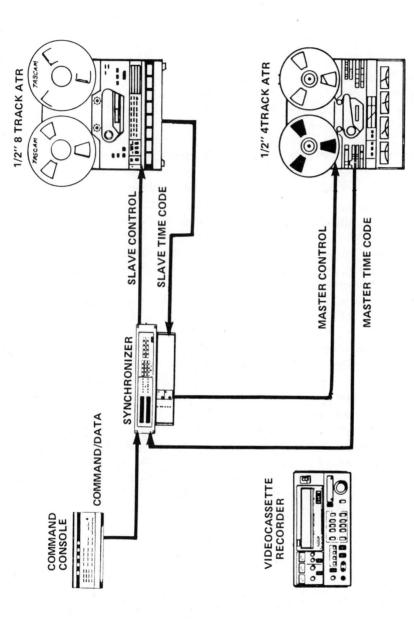

Fig. 7-8. The addition of master control and command console to the basic system configuration. Here sweetening is integrated with control track video editing.

taneously. This configuration, pictured in Fig. 7-9, would add the advantage of allowing synchronized program video when building from 4-track sources or when mixing directly to the 4-track.

The upgrade path for the producer with the control track editor is similar. Adding a control console is the first logical move, but unfortunately it does not readily integrate with the video editing system. Since only one controller (the synchronizer or the video editor) can control the VTR at any time, the system connections must be interchanged between video editing and the two shown in Fig. 7-7. This system now has the ability to do time code accurate edits from video cassette to ATR or between 4-track and 8-track, but sync audio for video edits still cannot be accurately reproduced in postedit sweetening. Adding another synchronizer eliminates some of the reconfigurations and provides three machine sync, giving program picture during building and mixing.

Another configuration of the same equipment, shown in Fig. 7-10, slaves both ATRs to the record VTR acting as a time-code-only master. This gives more centralized control during video editing and automates punch-in for the ATRs, but it adds little else in increased functionality.

For the case of the time code editor, adding only a control console may have little value. Adding a second synchronizer module as well, shown in Fig. 7-11 puts both ATRs simultaneously on-line in a code-locked, editing environment. This system has nearly ultimate versatility, with the one drawback that control is distributed between two consoles. The operator must interact with two logical systems and often perform duplicate functions, e.g. time code entry, on both keyboards.

Once a synchronizer controller is installed, additional audio or video decks can be included in the system by adding additional synchronizer modules for each, allowing synchronizing and control of all machines simultaneously, or by acquiring additional interfaces for the existing synchronizer modules and swapping the synchronizer modules to the decks involved in the current operation.

COMPUTERIZED SYNCHRONIZER CONTROL

In Chapter 5 the internal workings of a synchronizer as a microcomputer were discussed. Also mentioned was the ability to communicate with that microcomputer through RS-232 or RS-422 serial data links, and how synchronizer controllers use that link to manage their subordinate synchronizer modules. Since the communication interface is an industry standard and the communication protocols are published by the synchronizer manufacturers, the possibility of externally controlling a synchronizer module is

124

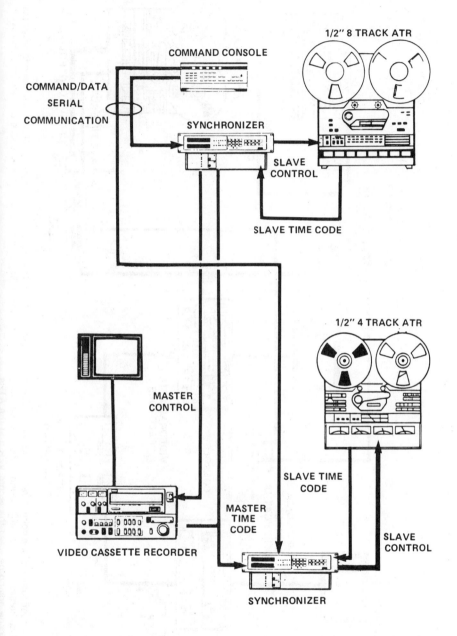

1/2" 8 TRACK ATR

COMMAND CONSOLE

COMMAND/DATA
SERIAL
COMMUNICATION

SYNCHRONIZER

SLAVE
CONTROL

SLAVE TIME CODE

1/2" 4 TRACK ATR

MASTER
CONTROL

SLAVE TIME
CODE

MASTER
TIME
CODE

SLAVE
CONTROL

VIDEO CASSETTE RECORDER

SYNCHRONIZER

Fig. 7-9. Adding a second synchronizer to the system with no editor puts three decks under control of the command console and allows time code editing between the VTR and two ATRs.

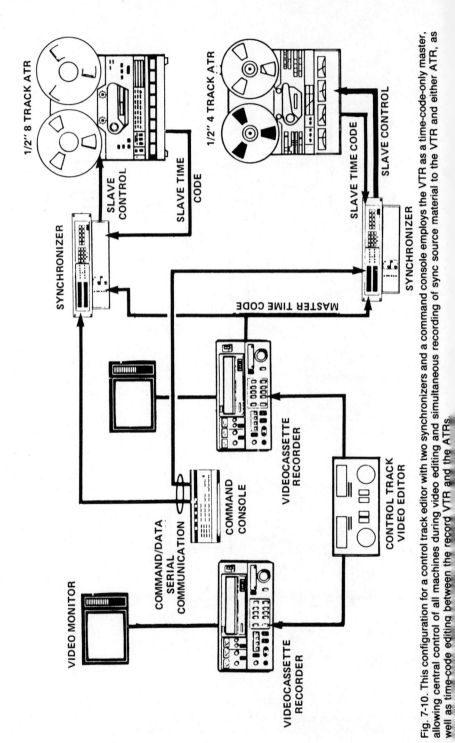

Fig. 7-10. This configuration for a control track editor with two synchronizers and a command console employs the VTR as a time-code-only master, allowing central control of all machines during video editing and simultaneous recording of sync source material to the VTR and either ATR, as well as time-code editing between the record VTR and the ATRs.

126

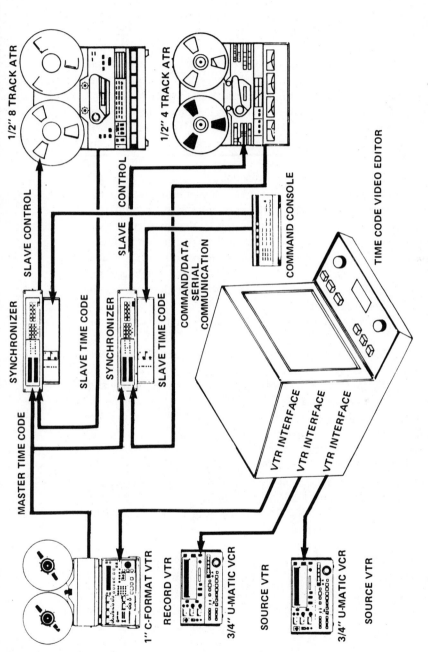

Fig. 7-11. Slaving two ATRs to the record VTR in a time-code editing system puts all machines under time code lock for any type of synchronized transfer.

readily exploited. Personal computers are a potential tool for controlling synchronizers.

Almost every personal computer has or can have an RS-232 interface installed, giving it hardware compatibility with the communications interface of a synchronizer. That is to say, the personal computer can send data to the synchronizer and can read data the synchronizer sends back. Establishing this hardware communication is often not as simple as plugging this cable into that hole. Often some hardware savvy is required to ensure that the send data lines are connected to the receive data lines, that handshaking is properly actuated, that baud rates match, and so on. This kind of help is readily available.

Once the devices are successfully linked and are talking to each other, implementing control functions is a programming task and anyone with a basic knowledge of programming is a candidate to control his synchronizer. This is not to say that just anyone can program in all the functions of a Softouch. Synchronizer manufacturers have developed sophisticated software to execute sophisticated functions. On the other hand, building basic capabilities and perhaps some special-purpose functions is well within reach of the nonprofessional programmer.

Sending commands for primitive machine motion control and synchronizing is the first step. Reading time code follows. Executing multiple-machine edit events would be a more serious undertaking. Those with some computer experience may already see the potential for applications in their operations. Here are a few suggestions to set imaginations in gear.

Use your computer to log source materials. The goal is to speed up and standardize the process of logging either video or audio source material. The computer is programmed for three interactions with the synchronizer: PLAY, STOP, and READ time code. The operator has two keys on the personal computer designed for PLAY and STOP and another two for READ and LOG. The operator uses PLAY and STOP while listening and/or watching the material. At the start of a take the operator presses the designated READ key and the computer gets the time code from the synchronizer. At the end of the take, the operator presses LOG, whereupon the computer requests the scene number, take number, and a descriptor such as OK, EXCELLENT, FALSE START, SCRIPT ERROR, etc. The computer records the data for the take along with the time code and then prepares for the next take. The logged data may be saved to disk, printed, or edited as necessary.

Use your computer to find and access sound effects from a data base. The goal is to streamline access to a large library of sound effects. Suppose the sound effects library is transferred from records, cassettes, or 1/4" to one time-coded 4-track tape. During or following the recording, the time code, track numbers, and effect descriptions are entered into a computerized data base. A simple program could, at the operator's request, access the data base to extract the time code and track number of the requested effect, tell the operator to punch up track X, send the time code to the synchronizer to cue to the effect—generally getting things ready to roll for listening or editing. If integrated with a standard database management program the effects data base could be categorized, indexed, and cross-referenced for easy access to groups of effects classified by sound source, tonal qualities, durations, or just about anything.

This principle, the small computer controlling synchronizers, is appearing both in commercial products and specialized systems throughout the industry. A new generation of editing systems in both the video and audio worlds is utilizing this architecture. The operator interface and the editing intelligence are implemented in a microcomputer, the microcomputer communicates with synchronizers or similar independent devices through serial data links, and the synchronizer or a similar device handles all the direct machine control. In essence, a new or specialized editing or sweetening system controller can be built without designing and fabricating custom interfaces for every type of VTR or ATR to be used in the system.

Examples of this type of product were recently introduced by Calaway Engineering and Alpha Automation. Calaway's video editor uses an IBM Personal Computer for the editing console and central intelligence, communicating with either Calaway's proprietary interfaces or synchronizers all through serial lines. Designed primarily for audio work, the Alpha Automation sweetening/editing controller is structured similarly, relying on Adams-Smith synchronizers as the machine interface elements.

An interesting example of a special-purpose system created in this mold was shown by Steve Waldman and Audio Kinetics in 1983. A booklet was printed listing sound effects and descriptions, with a bar code associated with each effect listing. The producer searching for sound effects peruses the book and selects effects by passing a light pen over the adjacent bar code. The light pen signals pass to a computer which compiles a list of the selected effects. The computer is also connected to a synchronizer and ATR. For listening, recording, or editing, the computer finds and plays the effects by referring to a stored table of time code numbers, identifying the location of the effects on the ATR.

Even the established video editor manufacturers are beginning to recognize the beauty of using synchronizers in this type of configuration as machine interface units. Just as CMX has done for so long, many suppliers are adopting the distributed intelligence approach to building high-power video and audio editing and sweetening control systems.

Chapter 8

Sweetening Techniques

---

sound \ ′ saúnd \ *n* **1** : the sensation produced in the ears by certain vibrations or waves conveyed by the atmosphere or other medium **2** : the combination of spoken words, music, and sound effects that helps to create and enhance a video program's meaning and impact

With a basic understanding of the sweetening process and the hardware tools available, the next issue must be the techniques of sweetening. It would be impossible to present an absolutely comprehensive "how-to" of sweetening, so this chapter discusses selected issues of technique related to the principal software elements of a soundtrack (Fig.8-1). On-camera dialog, narration, and sound effects are addressed; music is saved for a chapter of its own. The techniques presented are generally most relevant to selection of materials and the track-building process, but occasionally the comments drift off into other topics. If the sections herein seem disjointed, accept each on its own merits, as an independent pointer for use when circumstances dictate.

ON-CAMERA DIALOG

If the program you are sweetening has on-camera, "lip-sync" dialog, there are several ways it can be treated during the track-

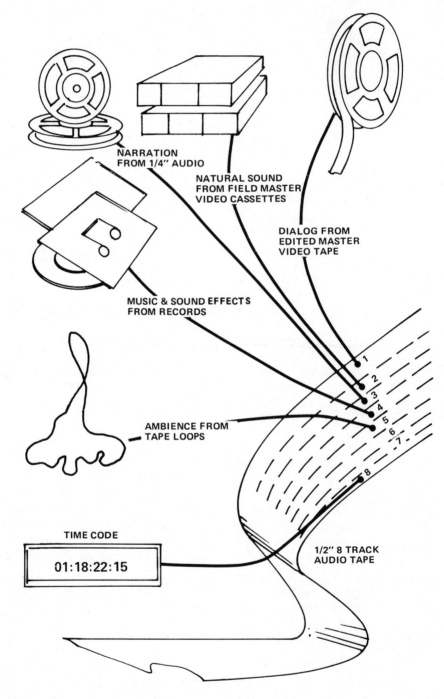

NARRATION
FROM 1/4" AUDIO

NATURAL SOUND
FROM FIELD MASTER
VIDEO CASSETTES

DIALOG FROM
EDITED MASTER
VIDEO TAPE

MUSIC & SOUND EFFECTS
FROM RECORDS

AMBIENCE FROM
TAPE LOOPS

TIME CODE

01:18:22:15

1/2" 8 TRACK
AUDIO TAPE

Fig. 8-1. The materials come from a variety of sources and all end up on the multitrack during the track-building step.

building process (Fig. 8-2). If you are sweetening in the conventional manner, i.e., you have done a laydown of the audio track from your videotape edited master (see "laydown" in Chapter 2), then your dialog will already exist on a predetermined channel of the multitrack recorder. A conventional laydown of the dialog is the simplest and most cost-effective manner for placing the dialog on the multitrack, because it was edited along with the video; however, it may not provide you with the degree of control necessary for treatment of more complex situations.

If, on the other hand, you edit your programs in an off-line environment and prebuild and sweeten the audio prior to on-line assembly and mastering, the dialog tracks must be assembled separately; the process is identical to assembling the video. This requires the use of a computerized editing controller such as the CMX Edge, 340X, etc., or an intelligent controller like the Cipher Digital Softouch or Shadowpad (Fig. 8-3). The edit decision list, or its event source and record numbers, are used in this assembly process.

Assembling the dialog in this manner offers the greatest degree of control, in terms of being able to split the dialog to individual

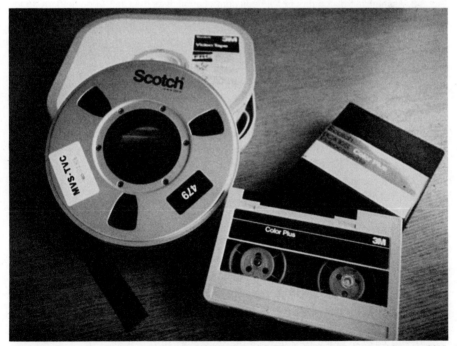

Fig. 8-2. On-camera dialog is taken from the original field masters, which are either on 3/4″ video cassette or 1″ video tape. If the dialog tracks are not recorded to the multitrack during the laydown step, they must then be assembled (much like video is assembled) to the multitrack.

Fig. 8-3. Assembling dialog requires an edit controller such as the CMS Edge (left), or an intelligent synchronizer controller such as the BTX/Cipher Digital Softouch (center).

tracks. This is particularly useful if your program was shot "theatrical-style," with master, over-the-shoulders, and closeups of individual characters. Splitting the dialog tracks to two or more channels allows much more control over volume and equalization. For instance, if your scene has two people talking to one another, you can set the volume and EQ separately to give each actor the correct audio "flavor," thus saving many hours during the final mix. Constantly riding the pots during the mix, to smooth out volume and EQ differentials from the original field masters, can be a rather tedious process.

Using the hardware device termed a *noise gate* may help cut some of the background noise inherent in punching out during the assembly of the dialog to the multitrack. However, the use of the noise gate may also cut out some of the background presence associated with the original tracks, thus leaving audio holes in the track where this presence is absent. If that is the case, the presence tracks will have to be added in the form of presence loops, which are described in more detail later in this chapter.

If you have decided to build the dialog tracks in this manner, i.e., assembling them one-by-one from the field masters to separate tracks, it may be necessary to do a *dialog premix*; vacant tracks may become precious. If an 8-track audio recorder is being used, then three of the tracks will be reserved, one for the audio track from the EM, one for the time code, and one for the final mix. Many engineers prefer to leave the track next to the time code channel vacant to alleviate the possibility of crosstalk from the code. Our tests with the TASCAM 58 proved this to be unnecessary, so long as the time code is recorded at -7 dB. It should be noted that the available tracks rapidly disappear when using an 8-track ATR; you won't often have the luxury of vacant tracks unless your program is very simple. A dialog premix combines the multiple tracks of dialog on one channel of the multitrack, freeing one or several channels for sound effects, narration, music, etc.

Assembling dialog to the multitrack may require implementing a video editor such as a CMX or other edit controller that has built-in audio/video switching capability. In order to record the dialog to the multitrack, it will have to be edited much like videotape is edited, which requires audio switching. The multitrack ATR must be configured as the record machine, and the 3/4" video cassette machine or 1" VTR containing the field masters must be configured as a source machine. Using a synchronizer with an intelligent "front panel" controller (such as the Cipher Digital Softouch or Shadowpad, the Adams-Smith Event/Edit Controller, or the Sony Syncmaster) will provide the capability necessary to assemble dialog using an edit list as the source for the events. These controllers, having intelligence equal to video editing computers such as the CMX Edge, will accomplish the audio assembly task very efficiently.

Dialog assembly in this fashion has its advantages and disadvantages. The first advantage may be in cost savings if you don't master the video in your facility. Preassembling the audio track and sweetening it (by adding all necessary music, narration, and effects), and then mixing back to a compatible, time-coded medium such as 1/2" 4-track, means that you are done with the project once the video has been mastered. This saves the time and expense of audio laydown. Another advantage of assembling the audio to the multitrack, in addition to saving one generation by bypassing the EM-to-multitrack laydown step, is the degree of control that is offered. It is much easier to split dialog tracks, performing EQ and volume changes as necessary.

The disadvantage of preassembling the dialog or program audio from the field masters is that it almost doubles the work. The audio is edited simultaneously with the video during the mastering process when you edit your programs in an on-line environment. Hence the easiest process is to edit all of the program audio with the video, then do a laydown from the EM, then sweeten in the conventional manner.

An additional problem encountered in preassembling the dialog or program audio is computer/media compatibility of the Edit Decision List (Fig. 8-4). If you have done your off-line editing on a CMX Edge or 340-type system, your EDL will be on an 8" floppy disk. If you've used an ISC it will be on a 5 1/4" floppy, etc. If you have "paper edited" your program, your EDL will be on 8 1/2-by-11 cellulose. It is safe to assume that none of the intelligent synchronizer controllers will have media compatibility with your EDL, so you have two choices. The first is to enter each event manually through the keypad on the controller, or to use the serial interface and read in the list through another computer that has media compatibility with your edit controller.

On the other hand, if you are editing in an on-line environment such as interformat 3/4" to 1", the process is somewhat simplified by the fact that you will have two available audio tracks to which you can record audio. You can record narration or music for cutting the video and also use one audio channel to record the ambient sounds directly from the 3/4" field masters. This process will greatly simplify the track-building process as well; you can then

Fig. 8-4. Compatibility of edit decision lists (EDL) can be a problem. Pictured on the left is a CMX 8" floppy disk, a paper print-out on the right, and a CMX punched paper tape in the rear. Dialog could be autoassembled if the list were loaded into a CMX machine, but it would have to be entered manually (through the keypad) into a Cipher Digital or Adams-Smith synchronizer.

lay down both audio channels from the 1″ directly to two channels of the multitrack ATR, thus saving some of the steps necessary to build tracks. During the track-building process, you will only have to add music, background presence, or other material that was not built during the on-line video editing stage.

One final note on laydown is in order. If you have noise reduction equipment such as dbx or Dolby, this is a good time to use it, especially if you have edited from audio cassette. It is important to note that the signal must be encoded and decoded each time it is recorded. This means that if you encode with dbx between the videocassette audio channel and the multitrack, and thus have an encoded audio track on the multi-track ATR, then you will have to decode the signal during each rerecording step. It should not be copied in its encoded form.

The tried-and-true process of sweetening dictates that the audio be assembled with the video, then laid down to the multitrack. Although this method may not offer the greatest degree of control, it is obviously the easiest and probably the most cost-effective in terms of labor.

FIXING AND REBUILDING

More often than we producers care to admit, master tapes come back from the field with poorly recorded audio and dialog that is unacceptable for use in the finished program. Unacceptable audio can occur for a variety of reasons, including actors who were recorded off-mic, radio frequency interference (RFI) from wireless microphones, or background sounds such as traffic, conversation, etc., that "drown out" the dialog. Another constant source of nuisance is hum or similar electronically induced noise, such as your less-than-favorite radio station picked up through an improperly shielded mic cable. All of these things can happen to even the most professional production crew.

What can be done? Simple—rebuild the audio.

Most Hollywood-scale feature productions use various techniques for rebuilding dialog tracks, even though they may have been recorded acceptably on location. Most network TV shows only replace on-camera dialog if it unusable for any of the above-mentioned reasons. With a large-scale Hollywood crew, which is very expensive, it is often more cost-effective not to do extra takes of a scene if the sound mixer doesn't think they got clean audio. The old adage, "They'll fix it in post," always stands true, so they "loop it."

The technique of replacing on-camera dialog has two frequently used terms: looping and ADR. The term *looping* was coined because

Fig. 8-5. Synchronizers such as the Cipher Digital Softouch have a sequence that can be programmed into the unit's "soft keys"; this allows for automatic dialog replacement (ADR).

an editor physically constructed two loops, one of the picture, the other of the original audio track. The picture loop was loaded on a projector and the dialog loop was loaded on a "dubber-unit", a sprocketed magnetic-film playback unit. A fresh piece of magnetic-film recording stock was hung on a record machine, which was also interlocked with the picture and original dialog track. The dialog editor would supervise the "looping session" as the actor would rerecord the dialog.

Early in the 1970s, technology helped automate the process, hence the term *automatic dialog replacement*, or *ADR*. Both techniques are virtually the same and both yield the same end result: a new dialog track. When using film, it is possible to make physical loops with both the picture and sprocketed magnetic track. Videotape, however, cannot be cut into a physical loop, so the process must be automated by using SMPTE time code as the reference.

The technique of ADR is simple, given the appropriate equipment (Fig. 8-5). Using a synchronizer with a front-panel controller, the in and out points of the scene are marked with time code cues. The synchronizer will also control the audio tape recorder onto which the new dialog will be recorded. The Cipher Digital Softouch has a feature called "soft keys" that make the process quite simple.

Cue tones in the form of beeps are fed to the talent through the same headphones he or she is using to listen to the original dialog tracks. The beeps precede the cue point by several seconds. The talent watches a video monitor and listens to the original track and says the dialog—hopefully in sync. Replacing dialog requires a certain skill level, which takes practice. Most Hollywood talent, at least those who work frequently in features or television, have developed these skills. Many actors and actresses who work primarily in industrial or educational television may not have experience with ADR.

NARRATION

Building the narration tracks on the multitrack recorder present some of the same problems as assembling dialog; so does music when the video was edited to the music, such as in a montage. The typical video program that uses narration does so by having the visual cut to narration that is initially laid down on the EM from 1/4" audio tape. If this is the case, then the natural audio from the field masters (usually ambience) will have to be recorded to the multitrack during the appropriate phase of the track-building process. If you have recorded the narration to the EM in this fashion and don't care about the generational loss derived from the EM-to-multitrack laydown, then this method is the most expedient and cost-effective.

If you don't want to incur the generational loss from the laydown, then you have several options. The first and simplest is "hot rolling" the narration from the original 1/4" to the multitrack, attempting to synchronize it as closely as possible with the narration used for editing. This method will provide the least generational loss, but if the visuals were tightly edited to the narration, sync may be a problem.

If your sweetening and editing bay are one and the same, another option is to build the tracks on the multitrack recorder as you edit. For example, if you have a standard chase-mode synchronizer which is following the time code on the EM, wherever the EM goes the multitrack is sure to follow. This process allows you to record each of the audio elements as you need them to the appropriate channels on the multitrack, saving not only the generational loss but also the task of spotting and track-building, because you are building as you edit, in the on-line environment.

The first step when you are editing to narration thus becomes laying down the narration track to a predetermined channel on the multitrack recorder, from the narration 1/4". Then, as you edit the video to the narration, you enable the record function on another channel, making sure you place the already recorded narration channel in "sync" or safe mode so that you don't erase the narration. As you edit the video, you record the program audio from the field masters, giving the natural ambience for the scene. This also saves a step during the track-building process. If you were editing to music, the steps would be identical.

Building the audio tracks while you edit (Fig. 8-6) is obviously the most efficient procedure in terms of labor, because you won't have to spot the tracks and build them later. You are adding all of the materials as you use them during editing.

If you don't have the luxury of having your sweetening equipment in your on-line bay, or if all of your editing is accomplished in an off-line mode, then you will have to integrate the narration and the software elements conventionally during the track-building process. With narration, the best and most accurate method is to time code it on the original 1/4", by recording originally on 1/2" 4-track, or by bumping it to that machine and simultaneously recording time code and making a dub on video cassette. If you are using a time-code, EDL-management computer and make a list event out of each narration cue, then the process of reassembling the narration to the multitrack machine is a simple process with complete frame accuracy. If this method is the one you select, then all of the advantages and disadvantages illustrated under the dialog

Fig. 8-6. Music, narration, and sound effects all must be recorded to the multitrack machine. Here Fred Hull creates an event, using the CMX Edge as the master machine controller.

Fig. 8-7. Sound effects libraries, also available on record albums, are another very important element for audio sweetening.

assembly section of this chapter will apply.

If the timing of the narration doesn't require frame accuracy, then the simplest manner in which to build the narration tracks is to hot roll the narration directly from the 1/4″ master to the multitrack. Using the digital counter on the multitrack will provide cues for the process that should allow for very close duplication of the timing made during the editing of the video.

SOUND EFFECTS LIBRARIES

Aside from the natural sound effects recorded on video tape along with video footage, the principal source of sound effects is libraries (Fig. 8-7). Many sound effects libraries are commercially available; a reasonable investment can supply quite a variety of common effects. In evaluating libraries for purchase, the selection and variety of effects plus the documentation are dominant criteria, with audio fidelity following. Documentation is very important because descriptive, indexed, cross-referenced listings can save valuable time in finding the best effect for a situation.

One of the most comprehensive sound effects libraries available is from Network, boasting more than 12,000 sound effects on 87 albums, ranging from every type of footstep imaginable through every animal sound known to man. The catalog accompanying the library is about 480 pages long, with both sequential and alphabetical indexes. It is by far the most complete commercially available library that we have found. The Network sound effects library costs $950 complete or $22 per individual record. If you don't require such a diverse selection of effects, you may not need this complete a library.

Bainbridge (Van Nuys, California) and EFX (Minneapolis, Minnesota) are two smaller libraries that may suit your needs very well. Consisting of six or seven albums each, both of these libraries have many of the most often used effects; owning one or both will provide you with more than "the basics." Valentino also has a good sound effects library consisting of about 30 albums, one album of which is completely filled with laughs. Typically, sound effects albums are purchased with a buy-out provision, which means that the $10 to $20 fee per album is complete, with no costs or per-use license fees.

It should be noted that most effects are of little use when recorded on albums, except for background presence material. This is because most effects will have to be "edited in," i.e., synchronized to match the picture during the track-building process. LP records are a good, high-fidelity, inexpensive distribution medium for sound effects, but chances are good that once you have located the desired effect you will have to transfer it to another medium, perhaps even a time coded medium such as video cassette, in order to lay it over to the multitrack machine. Purchasing the library on 1/4" audio tape is more desirable for cuing, in that you can "hot roll" the effect to the multitrack, but having the library on linear audio tape makes finding and auditioning the desired effect more difficult. Soon several sound effects libraries will be available on compact disk: with the library in a computer data base, search and play will be a matter of a few keystrokes on an IBM PC or similar computer.

As described in the next section, you can easily accumulate effects of your own that will better represent the type of projects you typically produce. If you take the time to record good effects in the field when you're on a shoot and then transfer them to a medium such as 1/4" audio tape or video cassette, after a period of time you will have a library of your own "most often used effects."

CREATING SOUND EFFECTS AND PRESENCE

Sometimes the "perfect" effect just can't be found in a library, at least not in your library, so one must be created (Fig. 8-8).

Rumor has it that the laser gun sound effects for *Star Wars* were created, not with a real laser weapon, but by hitting the guy wires of a large transmission antenna. Tricks can be played with recorded sound effects by varying the speed of a tape recorder: doubling, halving, or (in the case of most dc capstan servo-controlled machines) making small adjustments.

Creating sound effects, especially background presence, may require building or integrating several effects on a multitrack ATR. For example, background presence for a scene shot in a hospital may require a combination of pages (*"Dr. Abrams, please call your office"*), telephone rings, voice murmur, typewriters, etc. All of these effects, whether recorded live or obtained from libraries, must be recorded to a multitrack and then mixed down to a single channel.

Upon reviewing most of the sound effects libraries now available, you'll find that single effects such as telephone rings and typewriters all exist individually, but finding the right combination of these to make a background presence loop for a given scene is very difficult. The amount of each individual effect needed to create an appropriate loop will vary greatly, depending on your scene. Obviously, if your scene takes place in a large telemarketing "boiler room", you will require much more phone ringing and chatter (murmur) than for a one- or two-person office.

To create a background loop for a boiler room, the first thing that you must determine is the size and activity of the room that

Fig. 8-8. Material for creating sound effects and background presence loops comes from a variety of sources, including audio from field video masters, sound effects record albums, 1/4" tape, and audio cassettes.

Table 8-1. Library Samples.

Library	Effect	Album/Category	Side	Cut
Network	Office Atmoshpere (has chatter, phones, etc.)	9	2	3
Brainbridge	Electric Typewriter	2	1	6
EFX	Electronic Phones	Machines	2	5
Valentino	Intercom Buzz	20	A	4
Brainbridge	Paper Crumple	3	2	20
EFX	Business Discussion	People	1	2
Network	Photocopier	9	6	12
EFX	Computer Keyboard	Machines	1	2

you want to portray, and the length of the loop required to fill the scene. If you build a physical loop, the duration is obviously unlimited, but loops often tend to sound like loops because certain distinctive sounds are heard over and over again. For this example we will assume that we are creating the ambience of a very large telemarketing department of 50 or more telephone salespeople, plus many clerical workers, etc. We will also assume that the shot was recorded MOS (without sound), or that a spokesperson was miked with a lavalier that picked up little ambience. One point regarding production audio worth emphasizing is that it is always most desirable to have as little natural ambience as possible, attempting to maximize the fidelity and clarity of the on-camera dialog and leaving the addition of the necessary ambience to postproduction sweetening, where you can realize the most control over the audio elements.

After ascertaining the size and length of the presence track, typically done during the spotting session, the next step in the process is to pull the catalogs or albums from the sound effects libraries that you have available. Each library has a selection of various effects necessary for the presence track. Of course, the more libraries that you own or have access to, the wider the selection of materials you will have available.

A review of our libraries at The Visual Communications Group, Inc., yielded the selections for the boiler room presence track listed in Table 8-1.

Once you've gathered the necessary elements, the next step is to build the unit on a multitrack recorder. Since the track being discussed here is rather complicated in terms of the number of elements, it would be most desirable to record the various elements on an 8-track recorder, filling all eight tracks. These could then be mixed down "wild," that is, without synchronization, to 1/4" audio tape, a video cassette, or even a high-quality audio cassette.

Start by hanging a reel and leadering the beginning, or setting the digital counter to zero. Then, one by one, lay over the effects to their predetermined channels on the multitrack. The digital counter on the machine is particularly useful for back-timing the start point. With a stopwatch, time the duration from the end of the previous cue to the start of the cue that you will be recording. When using the Network library, use the verbal slate as a reference.

Next, back up the multitrack recorder the appropriate number of seconds representing the duration between the cues on the album. The number on the digital counter will represent a negative number of seconds. Set the needle down on the album near the end of the preceding cue, from which point you made your timing. When the cue ends, start the multitrack recorder and drop it into the record mode. The effect should start when the counter reaches zero. If not, start over, making the appropriate adjustment to the amount you back-timed the multitrack. This technique of back-timing also works very well for recording music cues during the track-building process.

Once you've laid down the first cue, go back and verify that it was in fact recorded and that the start point is accurate. Then place the first channel, which you just recorded, in the sync mode and the next channel in the ready or record mode. Repeat the process for each additional effect. In the event that the effect that you lay down isn't long enough for the duration of the total presence track, such as the photocopier effect, repeat the process, resetting the digital counter to zero when the effect ends, until the cue lasts the entire length.

Although it is easier to lay down a short effect a number of times, as described above, you could also create a physical loop on a 1/4" ATR, or use the pause feature on an audio cassette machine to duplicate the effect, to yield the necessary duration for the overall presence track (Fig. 8-9).

Once you have recorded all of the necessary elements for the presence track and have mixed it to another medium, you will then have to lay it back to the multitrack ATR in its appropriate position, determined during the spotting session. As noted previously, you should premix as much as possible during the track-building process, that is, fading up the presence track to the proper background level at the beginning of the scene and fading it out at the end of the scene. This premixing will make the final mix a much simpler and more refined process.

An additional note about your custom-made effects and presence loops might be in order here. Since a great deal of work is involved in creating these effects, save them for future use. Saving both the multitrack version (so it can be remixed for a different scene) and the 1/4″ will greatly enhance your own library over the long term. Transferring the SFX to audio cassette is also a good practice. You can easily run the loop for several minutes, or however long you think you might need it, then save the cassette in your library.

Of course, you don't have to make use of a sound effects library to create individual effects or background presence loops. You can record everything you need by going out in the field with a recorder and gathering the effects yourself, but this is typically too costly and time consuming.

When recording effects and background presence in the field, a professional quality cassette recorder such as the Sony TCD-6C can be used very effectively (Fig. 8-10). The machine is portable and has built-in Dolby C so little generational loss or noise is incurred when "bumping", i.e., transferring to another medium for editing or mixing. Cassette recorders are also particularly useful

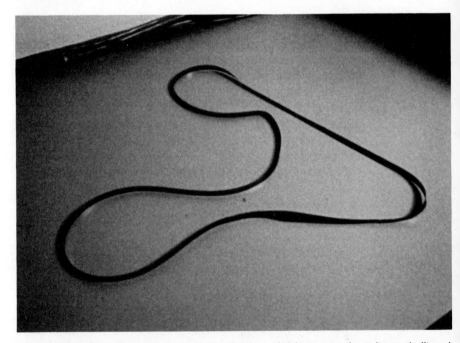

Fig. 8-9. Background presence can be recorded to a 1/4″ loop once the units are built and mixed; sometimes the repetitious nature of the loop can be discernible to the audience, however. The loop is created by recording to 1/4″ tape; then the beginning and end are razor-bladed together to form the continuous loop.

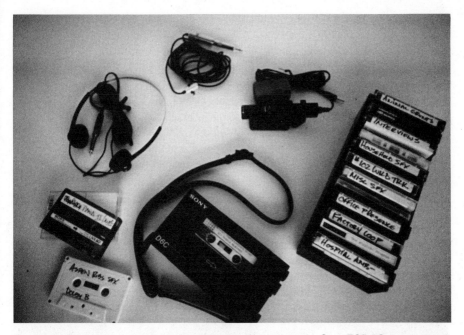

Fig. 8-10. With a high-quality audio cassette recorder such as the Sony TCD-6C, soon you will have the makings of your own sound effects library.

for recording nonsynchronous material such as interviews. These wild tracks or non-sync sounds are recorded more easily with a cassette than on a reel-to-reel Nagra. The Sony TCD-6C can also be used to record sync dialog if it is retrofitted with a crystal oscillator, as has been done by Skyline in Hollywood. This yields a *double-system*, meaning the audio is recorded on a different unit than the video. If the cassette recorder is used for this purpose, however, clap sticks for synchronizing the audio track to the picture must be used.

FOLEY

When replacing on-camera dialog with ADR, obviously all of the ambient sounds—including presence, footsteps, sound effects of the talent picking up props, door openings and closings, etc.—are eliminated from the track. All of these sounds also must be replaced. There are several methods for accomplishing this, and most often a combination of them is used.

Early in the 1940s, a sound mixer named George Foley at Warner Brothers Studios conceived a process to replace ambient sounds. While a scene was projected on a screen, several people would watch the scene and mimic the actions to recreate the ambient sound effects. They would gather all of the necessary props

147

from the scene, such as glasses, bottles, shopping carts, grocery bags, etc., gather a variety of shoes and floor types, and then reenact the action in front of open microphones that picked up all of the sounds (Fig. 8-11).

For example, if the on-camera talent was walking down a hallway with a wooden floor carrying a grocery bag, the Foley person would duplicate the action, attempting to match it precisely. The audio tracks derived from the Foley stage would then be edited by a sound effects editor and integrated into one of the sound effects tracks. Most network TV shows that are dubbed for foreign distribution are Foleyed, because the on-camera dialog will all be replaced with the foreign dialog tracks.

Setting up a scene for Foley, using video tape, is procedurally very similar to ADR. It requires the same equipment and approximately the same setup, although props and flooring are required. Smaller-scale productions such as industrials, educationals, and cable TV programs may not require the degree of ADR and Foley that network TV programs or feature films require, but there will

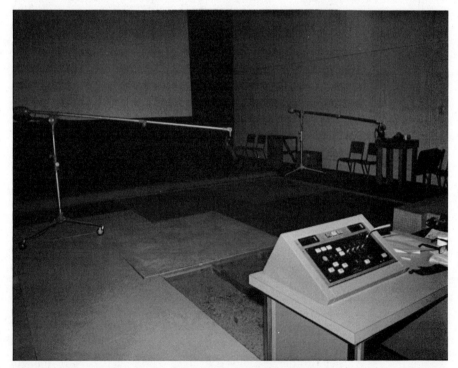

Fig. 8-11. "Foley" is the process of restoring natural sounds that are deleted as a byproduct of replacing on-camera dialog. When such sounds (footsteps and clothing rustle, for example) must be replaced, actors reenact on-screen motions on a "Foley stage" such as this one at Glen Glenn Sound.

Fig. 8-12. Most recent multitrack recorders have digital counters that make "back-timing" very easy.

be situations that require embellishment of certain on-camera sound effects. Furthermore, not all sound effects replacement must be Foleyed. Often simple sound effects editing, for replacing or adding such things as footsteps and door openings and closings, may be all that is required to add or replace on-camera effects.

USING PHONOGRAPH RECORDS

If you are using cues from a music or sound effects library, you need not transfer the cue to 1/4″ audio tape unless you must edit the cue with a razor blade, or if you are using the first cue on the side of the album and thus have no reference for back-timing. To back-time a cue, follow the procedure outlined earlier in this chapter, in the section on "Creating Sound Effects and Background Presence" (Fig. 8-12).

If by chance the music cue you wish to lay down is the first cut on the album, then obviously back-timing won't work because you have no reference from which to time the start point. Your options then are to try a couple of times in hit-or-miss mode, or to transfer the music cue over to 1/4″. To time the start point of the 1/4″ tape, find the beginning of the cue by rocking the reels back and forth in the edit mode and making a grease pencil mark at the appropriate point. Then leader the cue with leader tape that has timing markings printed on it. Use enough leader to give your machine time to get up to speed; usually a couple of seconds are enough, even when running at 15 ips.

Next, set up the 1/4″ machine with about a 2-second preroll and then start the multitrack machine 10 or 15 seconds in advance of the record point. The digital counter on the multitrack machine will read – 10 if you are using a 10-second preroll. If you have set the 1/4″ machine with a 2-second preroll, then press the play button on the 1/4″ ATR when the digital counter on the multitrack reads – 2 seconds. Don't forget to drop the multitrack machine into record on the appropriate channel.

SWEETENING AND MIXING FOR STEREO

With the explosion of music videos and the introduction of stereo TV, there will be an increasing demand for stereo mix tracks. Many local TV stations are now broadcasting in stereo; the FCC recently passed a regulation requiring cable TV systems to preserve the stereo signal when rebroadcasting the over-the- air signals. The process of mixing for stereo is no more difficult than mixing for mono, but increased demands are placed on the equipment and track availability. When using an 8-track ATR as the master machine, ping-ponging or submixing often will be required. Using a 16-track ATR or locking two or more multitrack machines also may become necessary.

The major requirement for tracks appears first during the track-building process. Every music segue or dissolve, instead of using two tracks, now will require four. If two tracks are being reserved for the stereo mix, and one is already consumed by time code, only one track is available for dialog, sound effects or background presence. An 8-track ATR is obviously insufficient unless premixing is done.

The solutions are neither simple nor cost-effective. The easiest solution is using a 16- or 24-track ATR, but most sweetening facilities have neither the financial resources nor the continuing requirement for more than an 8-track ATR. Locking up an additional multi-track machine is a viable solution—they can be rented or borrowed—but interfacing two or more multitrack machines requires additional hardware for the machines to be interfaced to the synchronizer. Most synchronizers, such as the Cipher Digital Shadow or the Adams-Smith require additional time code readers and machine interface modules, also not inexpensive to add to a sweetening facility. Probably the most cost-effective solution for occasional stereo projects is to rent or otherwise procure a 16-track machine. If your sweetening bay has an 8-track ATR and a 1/2″ 4-track ATR (for industry-wide compatibility, as described in

Chapter 6), then mixing to the 4-track becomes the most viable solution. The 4-track machine will have one track occupied with time code, one for a guard band, or spare track, and the other two for stereo mix left and right (Fig. 8-13).

Once the basic hardware constraints have been dealt with, the next obstacle becomes getting a good stereo mix. The key word in stereo is *separation*. Without a clear definition of left and right, going to the trouble of stereo is pointless (Fig. 8-14). There has always been a controversy regarding how much separation should exist between the left and right channels. This controversy arose in the recording industry, where many producers wishing to provide real separation were accused of producing "sterile" tracks. A common ground must be reached by mixing for good separation while maintaining the reality of the source material.

Mixing for stereo requires the sweetening bay to be set up so that the mixer, sitting between both speakers, can adequately hear the separation of the left and right channels. When mixing music that was previously mixed, either from a music library album or tape, maintaining that mix is simple: Just feed left to left, and right to right. When mixing mono tracks such as dialog, narration, or sound effects that require left or right separation, the pan pots on the mixing console are used. The pan pot is infinitely variable from full left, left-center, center right-center, to full right. By rotating the pan pot, the apparent source of the sound can be placed in any of these positions, or moved to match the action.

One of the more obvious applications for stereo mixing is to separate the dialog tracks of on-camera talent so that whoever is on the right side of the frame is mixed to stereo right and vice versa. This can be a tedious task, which is further complicated when the talent moves. Sound effects (presence material to some extent) can emit from a left or right position, such as a door opening or closing or a car driving across the screen from left to right. The door ef-

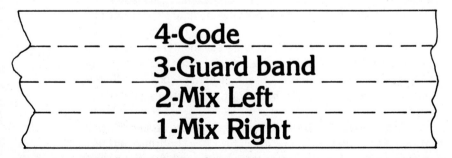

Fig. 8-13. Half-inch 4-track audio tape is best suited for stereo material because you can have time code on channel four with a guard band, plus stereo left and right on tracks one and two.

Fig. 8-14. Mixing for stereo requires that the mixing console be placed evenly between the left and right monitor speakers in the sweetening bay.

fect would merely require busing it to the appropriate mix channel, left or right, while the car traveling from left to right would require using the pan pot to follow it.

After mixing and approval of the mix of a stereo program, the next step in the process is the layback, which also requires some special attention. First of all and most obvious, the distribution medium must be two-channel, as are most 3/4″ and hi-fi video cassettes. If the master to which you intend to lay back is a 3/4″ cassette with the time code it must have for synchronization, however, you won't be able to lay back in stereo unless the 3/4″ cassette uses the third or "address" track for time code. (This is used on the Sony 800 series.) The ideal mastering medium for stereo/video mastering is 1″ video tape because of its two-channel audio capability, in addition to the time code channel. Once the stereo mix track is layed back to a 1″ edited master, then stereo dubs can be made on any two-channel video cassette; time code is no longer required for synchronization between the multitrack and edited master.

As with mixing in stereo for a record album, proper phasing is also important in sweetening audio for video. Improper phasing can cancel out a signal if it was miked or recorded out-of-phase. When played in mono, material present on both channels of a stereo mix will come back about 3dB louder—so be conservative with low-frequency material that is on two channels, because in a mono mode it may appear too loud. It is unlikely that improper phasing will occur during normal sweetening activities, so long as stereo material was not recorded "live" during the process.

CONFORMING MUSIC TRACKS

When sweetening sound tracks recorded live at concerts, etc., which must match edited video masters, the sweetening process becomes a little more complex. First, the original music tracks must be *conformed* to the edited video master (Fig. 8-15). It is most helpful if the original field video masters and the audio, multitrack masters were recorded with original time code, which saves the laborious task of computing offsets. Conforming the audio masters means editing the music tracks to match the video, much like the process of editing video tape. Ideally, the music tracks have already been mixed down to a time-coded medium such as 1/2" 4-track.

Conforming the music tracks is similar to the process of autoassembly with video tape. In fact, if the video tape was edited on a computerized video tape editing system such as CMX, an

Fig. 8-15. When editing video from live concerts, the original recordings off the multitrack ATRs must be conformed to the edited video master. Shown here is the interior of a mobile recording van (courtesy of MobilAudio, Inc.).

153

Fig. 8-16. Conforming master audio tracks, such as from a live recorded concert, requires the use of the video edit decision list. Ideally, the master time codes on both the video field sources and the multitrack music recordings are identical, thus saving the laborious step of calculating offsets.

edit decision list should exist, itemizing the source in and out times; these will correspond directly to the record in and out cues of the edited master. Again, if the original music tracks were recorded with time code identical to the video master's, the source times of the video will match those of the audio, making the conformation process as simple as video auto-assembly.

The mixed audio tracks are mounted on the 4-track 1/2″ ATR, which is locked to the master multitrack recorder (the one being used for sweetening, not the machines used for the original music recording) via the appropriate machine interfaces of the synchronizer or editing computer. If the conforming process is being done with a controller such as the Cipher Digital Softouch, instead of with an editing computer, then the time code events must be entered manually through the keyboard, instead of being read in from a floppy disk or paper punch tape. Event by event, the audio tracks are edited to the multitrack master, yielding audio tracks that match the edited video (Fig. 8-16).

Once the conformation has been accomplished (which might take days or weeks), other tracks such as audience presence, applause, etc., and any other necessary narration or announcements, are built like any show. Again depending on the complexity of the show, a 16-track ATR may be required for all of the stereo tracks, especially if segues are being used as transitions. The mix, if in stereo, must be performed as described above.

SWEETENING ON TAPE FOR FILM

With the "look" of film still being preferred by many producers over that of video tape, many programs are being originated on film and then transferred to video tape for various stages of electronic postproduction, which can be more efficient and cost-effective than traditional film editing. If the program was shot on film but then transferred to video tape for postproduction and final release, then no special steps are required for the sweetening process; because the program is now on video tape, the medium on which the picture originated doesn't matter (Fig. 8-17).

If, however, the program was edited on tape and the negative will be conformed to the edited video, or even if the picture was edited with traditional film methods, the audio can still be sweetened on tape and then transferred back to magnetic film or directly to an optical recorder. This layback requires an interface

Fig. 8-17. Shows produced on film can easily and efficiently be sweetened on tape, as long as the proper interface for the synchronizer is available to facilitate the interlock between the multitrack ATR and the film recorder.

Fig. 8-18. The PAP system at Glen Glenn Sound in Hollywood is interchangable between film and tape shows. Most network TV shows sweetened at Glen Glenn use a hybrid of magnetic film and multitrack audio tape. The shows are mixed, however, to 4-track magnetic film.

between the synchronizer, which is locked to the master ATR, and the film recorder.

Since the film standard is 24 frames per second and video tape is 30 frames per second, the synchronizer makes the conversion automatically. Audio tracks have no discrete frames, as film and video tape do. Most popular synchronizers, such as the Cipher Digital Adams-Smith, have interfaces to magnetic film transports. The actual sweetening process is identical to that of tape except that layback requires the additional interfaces and film transport equipment.

Many network TV shows, such as "Hill Street Blues," "St. Elsewhere," and "The A Team" utilize a hybrid sweetening process, in that the dialog tracks are transferred to and edited on 35mm magnetic stock, but the sound effects and music are built on a 16- or 24-track audio machine. This process, exemplified by Glen Glenn's PAP system (Fig. 8-18), uses both media in the final mix process, interlocking the multitrack with several film transports for source material such as dialog tracks. The final mix is recorded, in interlock through the synchronizer, to a 4-track 35mm magnetic film recorder.

SUMMARY

Once the basic sweetening skills and techniques have been acquired and refined, the art of sweetening is limited only by the creative imagination and the equipment needed to accomplish the task. Poorly recorded audio can be fixed and rebuilt, and unacceptable dialog can be replaced. An infinite variety of sound effects and background presence can be synthesized using prerecorded and original materials. Audio tracks can be sweetened and mixed for stereo and conformed to video masters of live events. Sweetening on tape can also be part of the electronic postproduction of film shows that have been transferred to video tape for more efficient and less expensive editing.

Chapter 9

Working with Music

mu • sic \ 'myü-zik \ *n* the art and science of combining
vocal or instrumental sounds or tones in varying melody,
harmony, rhythm, and timbre, especially so as to form
structurally complete and emotionally expressive com-
positions

Everyone, professional and viewer alike, recognizes the impact of
music on a program. In many productions music can help to make
or break the show. Music can heighten the informational content
and increase the emotional impact of a program, as well as integrate
the program and unify it. Music can be used to emphasize actions,
help define images, and ideas, reinforce characters, set time periods
and locales, and even suggest new meanings through interaction
with the visual program. By recalling past events, foreshadowing
future ones, and linking distinct visual elements, music provides
story continuity. This has been known to the Hollywood producers
since before the "talkies." Even just the pit piano in the early days
of film was considered extremely important. As soon as the
"talkies" were introduced, the music scores were right there with
the rest of the sound. Music can also fulfill some of the more mun-
dane tasks, in masking noises and filling in gaps which may be difficult or impossible to deal with in any other way.

Since a good sound track can infinitely enhance a mediocre program, music is one of the most important elements in the sweetening process. Of course, an original music score is the best for any production because the music can be composed to fit the mood of a scene or shot and can be written to bridge scenes or to fit neatly under narration or on-camera dialog. Budgets being what they are for most small-scale productions, however, library music is typically the only possibility. We will discuss the use of both.

In this chapter we will look at some of the considerations in planning music for your production. First we will look at some general planning guidelines. Then we will look at how these guidelines and considerations apply to using library music, make a survey of available music libraries, discuss original music, and evaluate the combination of library and original music. As in many other areas of production in general, there aren't a lot of hard and fast rules governing how music is used in any visual medium. There are some things that most producers would agree on and others they will never agree on. This chapter will probably not put an end to any of those arguments. However, it is hoped that shared experience and information will help to encourage the creative use of music.

PLANNING YOUR MUSIC TRACK

There can be many things to consider in a properly planned music track. Where to put music in the program, whether to use library or original music, the production plan and schedule, whether to edit picture to sound or score to picture, and—last but not least—how much all this will cost. These decisions need to based on your particular program, scheduling considerations, budgets, clients and/or other bosses, and personal taste.

Spotting Music

One of the first things to be decided on, is where and how much music to use. Although there are certainly no fixed rules here, the following points should be considered in making this decision.

1) The communication goals of the program.
2) The audience with whom the program is trying to communicate. Considerations include such things as age, sex, family status, profession, national or ethnic factors, etc.
3) The program's presentation style. Is it a Coke commercial or a training program? Are fast action and high-speed visuals being used, or is the audience motivated to pay attention on their own?
4) Budget and schedule considerations. Does the program

have to be on the screen in 2 days from start to finish, or is it a 6-month schedule? Do you have $100,000 budgeted for original or do you have $100 for the entire program, including special effects?

Thinking about these things ahead of time may help to make your decisions concerning music much easier. The most obvious places for music are usually the beginning and end, as well as otherwise difficult transitions. Some types of programs need music all the way through, such as most 2-minute image programs. Others, such as a 30-minute computer training program, may not need much music at all.

One common misconception is that if the program emphasizes training, music is not helpful. Many times this is a lazy approach. Most programs, training or otherwise, can be helped with careful insertions of music at selected points or scenes. It is helpful to think about other programs that you have seen, ones which you think work well. Evaluate them with respect to their sound track. Learn from other programs what music techniques work well and apply these ideas to your own productions.

Another way to think about where to put music is to decide where *not* to put music. Sometimes this can be more difficult but more beneficial. If you are unsure about a scene, try some music of a style you think might work and see if it helps the scene. Certainly there are many programs that do not need music all the way through. Restraint is part of the wisdom you need to acquire.

Try to pick or specify music for a particular scene that fits the mood of the scene, keeping in mind the intended audience. Some moods should be delicate, while others should be hard-driving and upbeat. Many times the mood needs to change at a transition between scenes, and sometimes it needs to change in the middle of a scene. This can be a very effective use of music. The music can change with the scene, or maybe it can foreshadow what is about to happen. It can help prepare the audience for what is to come, or make them tie that scene together with an earlier scene in the program. This can be done by selecting the proper style, tempo, and energy of the music. The same or similar theme can be used throughout the program to tie different scenes together. Maybe you use the music to tie different characters or locations together. The proper selection of music really gives you another valuable tool to help communicate with your audience. It would be a shame to not use it as effectively as possible.

Library or Original Music?

Many times there is really no decision to make here, especially in small-scale television productions. However, you should know what options are available. The sections that follow will give a more detailed explanation of cost and scheduling considerations. Normally, this decision needs to be made fairly early in the production schedule; knowing your options will help you make it.

Most producers would agree that original music scores are best for most programs. However, original scores cost more money, and take more or better planning. The impact to be gained from using an original score is great, but this can be somewhat scary for producers not used to using original music. (The cost of original scores have decreased in recent years with the advent of synthesizers, but more on that later.) When schedules and budgets are tight, library music is the only choice. When used properly, and with attention to detail, the music libraries can be very effective. There are many excellent libraries, and the more you know about what is available, the more effective you will be in using them.

There is an alternative to using just music libraries or just an original score. It is possible to have the best of both worlds. You can have original music for part of the program and library music for a part of the program. In this way you can gain the tremendous advantages of original music, and yet save money using music libraries. You can have the original music contain a theme for the beginning, end, and the more difficult transitions (or any other scene which may require special attention), and then use the music libraries for those sections which are easier to match moods, or where musical changes are not necessary. This can tremendously increase the impact of a program while helping to maintain the budget.

Your Production Plan and Schedule

It is important to plan your production schedule to include the music elements. If you are using library music, you need to schedule a time to spot your program and listen to music. If you are having your sound track done at an outside sound studio, then time needs to be scheduled for listening and assembling your sound track. This usually has to be coordinated with voice talent, and with the gathering together or specifying of sound effects and other elements of the sound track.

If you are using original music, then a composer must be selected and contacted. Production schedules must be worked out with the composer so he can schedule writing time, studio time, and musicians. Even before a shoot begins, the members of the production team must be contacted and made aware of the desired schedule. If there are problems with parts of the schedule, it is much easier to change them ahead of time than try to figure it out during production. If the schedule is subject to change, that fact should be communicated as well. Find out from each member of the production team how much time he would like to have for his job, and work the schedule to satisfy the most people. It is much easier for people to schedule a few days a month in advance than to make themselves available tomorrow. This especially applies to freelancers. Also, it is best to include the composer at the very beginning of the production. That way he or she may be able to give you ideas to help save time or money, and make the production schedule easier for everyone.

Visuals or Soundtrack First?

In the typical film tradition, the visuals are edited first; any music, effects and narration are added afterward. Many times this is the best way to approach the video medium as well. However, sometimes it is best to assemble the sound track first and edit the video to the sound track. If the later method is chosen, it would not be able to include lip-sync dialog. However, this could be added over an otherwise finished sound track.

In short, fast-moving scenes where the visuals are to be tightly synchronized with the sound track, it is usually best to assemble the sound track first. This makes the video editing take less time, and is the only option if you are using library music. Commercials generally are done this way if they involve music. This means that the scenes had to be storyboarded ahead of time. This is an absolute necessity if you are using original music, and is still desirable if using library music. Most other situations in video are best handled by having the music done to picture, whether library or original. Sometimes in longer programs both methods would be used, with each scene that requires music determining the best method for that scene. In shorter programs (under 15 minutes) this is usually not practical.

USING LIBRARY MUSIC

As mentioned above, there are benefits and disadvantages to using library music. However, once the decision is made to use library music, you need to know how to use it to its fullest advantage.

First, of course, is the selection of the music you will use and where you will use it. This should be decided by listening to the music, keeping the goals of the program in mind. It is best to select music that will fit the mood and tempo of a scene, without too much regard for the length of the musical piece. Length can sometimes be a problem, but it can be dealt with unless a scene or section is unusually long. As you are selecting music, it also is important to keep in mind whether the music will be under dialog or narration. If it is, then you must select music that won't compete with the voices. Music that competes with the voice draws your attention away from the dialog or narration when it is not supposed to. If it does compete, then the music may have to be mixed in at a fairly low volume level—which may make the music less effective than it needs to be.

After the music is selected, it is time to assemble the music into the sound track. This can be a tedious and moderately technical job, depending on the program. This is also the point where strict attention must be paid to timing considerations. For musical selections which are longer than the scene where they are being used, it is best to find the part of the selection which is closest to what you want. Then, in building the music track, fade the music in and out at the appropriate places. It is almost always best to premix the levels of music during the track-building process.

It there are two or three parts of the selection that work better than the other parts, the music selection can be transferred to 1/4" audio tape and edited to better suit the scene. If the music selection is somewhat too short for the scene, the music can be copied to 1/4" audio tape a couple of times. Then edit the 1/4" audio tape to repeat parts or all of the music selection to fit the timing of a scene. This works well with most library selections. However, you must be careful to make the edited music sound natural. This works best with music selections that do not change music keys or have tempo variations within the piece, unless the edits are done within a section where key and tempo are consistent. After editing where necessary, the music is then laid down to the multitrack ATR and assembled with the other elements of the sound track.

Many times, some amount of equalization to the music track can make it more effective. This can be done during the track-building process or during the mix. The music can be made to stand out more by brightening, such as adding 3 to 6 dB at 5000 to 8000 Hz. The music can sometimes be made to fit better around the dialog or narration by adding 3 to 9 dB at below 200 Hz. Experiment with equalization to help the music fit.

If you are using a recording studio and you are not synchronized with the video, you can expect to pay from $40 to $70 per hour to assemble your sound track. For studio or production houses that sync audio to 3/4" or 1" video, you can expect to pay from $50 to $150 per hour. If you do all of your audio work in a video production house, the rates vary even more; they start at $75 per hour and run up to $350 per hour, depending on the production house and what part of the country you are in. Most studio and production houses charge half the normal studio rate to listen to music from libraries. The "needle-drop" fees are discussed in the next section. Your total sound track budget is directly proportional to how much time you spend in the studio, which could range from a couple of hours to a couple of days. If you are able to do your audio work in-house, the only charges you have with music would be the needle-drop fees.

MUSIC LIBRARIES

"The whole is greater than the sum of the parts" is a great description of the elements necessary to produce a great program. As every producer knows, music libraries are one of the most essential ingredients of the sweetening process on any scale. A program is comprised of many elements, working in synergy, forming a whole, but music can make or break it (Fig. 9-1).

As we have noted, having an original musical score composed is the most desirable approach for any production. Since few of us can afford the luxury of using original music in most cases, how-

Fig. 9-1. Music libraries, of which there are over 25, are an essential ingredient in the audio sweetening process.

ever, we must turn to music libraries to enhance our programs. Announcers on the demos from most of the available music libraries will tell you, "Ours is the only library you will need to own, for all your production needs." That may or may not be the case, depending on what "your production needs" happen to be. If you are producing a series, or if all of your material follows the same general "look" (and sound), then possibly you may get away with owning one library, or even just a few albums within one library.

There are over 25 different sources for libraries currently available, most of them economically comparable. Some libraries are better and more versatile than others, but none that we have reviewed is bad, or without merit. Some of the bigger, more established libraries (such as DeWolfe or Valentino) are very broad in scope, offering hundreds of albums. Other libraries (such as Network, which has about 40 albums) are extremely popular and offer a good range for most "production needs" in today's environment, within the limited selection they may offer.

Every library offers some level of personal service, which is of great value when you have a particular music requirement but don't have the "right" album in-house. In that case, you'll want to call the library and express your needs, and have several albums (or tapes) sent for an audition, typically on an approval basis. This means you can send it back, at no charge, if you don't like it. All libraries will tell you that they are in the business of selling license fees, not selling albums. When you are trying to select a library or two for purchase, call up several and try to establish a personal relationship. Try to get a feel for how well that particular library can respond to your individual needs.

When selecting a library, you will encounter several different types of usage or license fee structures. The most common, and perhaps the oldest, is the standard *needle-drop* fee. Every time you "drop" the needle, you pay a fee ranging from approximately $50 to $100. If you have to make an edit to lengthen the cue, then you would pay two needle drops. Other libraries, such as Network, charge by the running minute of music used. These prices range from $50 for a minute or less, through $250 for 10 minutes, no matter how many different cues you have used. Most all libraries also offer a "yearly buy-out," whereby you pay a license fee based on your type of usage, e.g. broadcast or nonbroadcast, for a flat fee of approximately $2000—no matter how much music you use. This type of license fee greatly simplifies the paperwork required for license fees.

One of the most interesting libraries currently available is Soper Sound, from Palo Alto, California. As of early 1985, the library is available in album series from 1 through 10. One of the unique things about this library is the demo cassette tapes which are directly correlated to the catalog. You can preview the library by listening to the demo cassettes and looking through the catalog simultaneously. The announcer lists the category album and cut number so you can note selections that you like; then you can order the appropriate albums.

Another interesting feature of the Soper library is the Music-Selector™ computerized database management tool for performing library searches. The Music-Selector uses the Personal Filing System™ from Software Publishing Corporation and the Apple II or IBM PC, and has files for all of the selections in the Soper library. It also allows the user to add selections from other libraries. You use the Music-Selector by typing in key words that categorize the music, entering variables such as mood, tempo, desired duration of the cue, and instrumentation; the computer then does a search of the files and brings up a listing of the appropriate cues.

In gathering information for this section of the book, we surveyed via a questionnaire all of the music libraries that we could find using trade advertising and personal referrals as sources. We have compiled the chart shown in Table 9-1 as a reference to help you better understand the offerings of each of the libraries. A complete listing of the libraries is contained in Appendix B.

In addition to the questionnaire, we also sent a listing of music requirements for "The A-Typical Program." This was a mock program, listing requirements for a variety of cues to fit a wide range of visuals. Our objective was to test the individual libraries' searching services. To our surprise, only Soper, Valentino, NFL Films Music Library, and MusiCrafters responded with suggestions. All of the responses were excellent and it is difficult to rate the libraries based on them, since music selection is very subjective. Valentino, NFL Films, and Soper sent several albums and indicated their suggestions, while MusiCrafters sent a cassette with the selections prerecorded. The selections made by Musicrafters were very close to our personal tastes and the music was of very high quality. The others who responded did so with great care and all of the selections were useful.

Network Production Music of San Diego, California, is probably the most popular library in the United States in terms of use, but it is also one of the smallest in terms of albums. The music available from Network is of very high quality and very versatile, but is very much overused. We have encountered many situations where we have selected a cue for an opening montage from Network only to play it for the client and hear something like, "Well, isn't that

Table 9-1. Cross-Reference Index of Music Libraries.

Name:	Associated Production Music Bruton Music	Associated Production Music Conroy	Associated Production Music KPM	Associated Production Music Themes International	Comprehensive Video Supply Corporation	Creative Support Services or Repro-file™	DeWolfe Music Library, Inc.	MusiCrafters	Network Production Music, Inc.	NFL Films Music Library	Soper Sound Music Library	Themes/ ZM Squared	Valentino Production Music Library	Voyage Music Library
Contacts (by region):	Hollywood: John Osiecki / New York: Phil Spieller	Hollywood: John Osiecki / New York: Phil Spieller	Hollywood: John Osiecki / New York: Phil Spieller	Hollywood: John Osiecki / New York: Phil Spieller	—	—	Andrew Jacobs, Mitch Greenspan, Rick Lake and Fred Jacobs	Elena Morino	Michael Anderson	Doris Abelson	Harn Soper and Kathy Wolff	Terry Zakroff and Pete Zakroff	Tom Valentino, Joanne Rosen and Frank Valentino	Jim Diven and Keiko Takeda
Date of Inception:	1977	1955	1955	1955	—	1982	1940	1984	1978	1977	1978	1980	1932	1982
Where Music is Recorded:	London, England	London, England	London, England	London, England	—	Los Angeles	England	Philadelphia and New York	San Diego	Philadelphia, New York and Munich	San Francisco	Philadelphia and Los Angeles	Various	Los Angeles
Number of Albums/ Number of Yearly Additions:	280/ 40	150/ 10 to 20	325/ 40 to 50	48/ 10 to 20	16 (2 sets)	8/ 4	750/ 60	4/ 6	40/ 12	23/ 3 to 5	30/ 4 to 6	20/ 4 to 10	203/ 14	4/ 3 to 4
Number of Libraries Represented:	4	4	4	4	2	1 (6 on Needle Drop Basic)	4	1	1	1	1	1	1	1
Number of Composers Used:	Over 50	Numerous	Over 50	Numerous	—	3	Numerous	Numerous	Numerous	Numerous	8	Numerous	35	1 to 2

Table 9-1 continued.

Name:	Associated Production Music Bruton Music	Associated Production Music Conroy	Associated Production Music KPM	Associated Production Music Themes International	Comprehensive Video Supply Corporation	Creative Support Services or Repro-file™	DeWolfe Music Library, Inc.	MusiCrafters	Network Production Music, Inc.	NFL Films Music Library	Soper Sound Music Library	Themes/ ZM Squared	Valentino Production Music Library	Voyage Music Library
Available Formats:	33 RPM/ 7/12 2-Track/ 15 2-Track	33 RPM/ 7/12 2-Track/ 15 2-Track	33 RPM/ 7/12 2-Track/ 15 2-Track	33 RPM/ 7/12 2-Track/ 15 2-Track	24-Track	7/12 2-Track/ 15 2-Track/ Cassettes	33 RPM/ 7/12 2-Track/ 15 2-Track	33 RPM/ 7/12 2-Track/ 15 2-Track	33 RPM/ 7/12 2-Track/ 15 2-Track	33 RPM/ 7/12 2-Track/ 15 2-Track	33 RPM/ 7/12 2-Track	7/12 2-Track/ Cassettes	33 RPM/ 7/12 2-Track/ 15 2-Tracks	33 RPM/ 7/12 2-Track/ 15 2-Tracks
Masters Available for Special Mixes:	Yes	Yes	Yes	Yes	No	Yes	No	Yes	Yes	No	No	No	Yes	Yes
Demo Format/ Correlated to Catalog (Identifying Cue):	Cassette/ No	Cassette/ No	Cassette/ No	Cassette/ No	Record	Cassette/ No	Cassette./ Yes	Soundsheet and Cassette/ Yes	Record and Cassette/ Yes	Cassette/ Yes	Cassette/ Yes	Cassette/ Yes	Record and Cassette/ Yes	Record/ No
Phone Consultation Available/ Fee:	Yes/ No	Yes/ No	Yes/ No	Yes/ No	No	Yes/ No	Yes/ No	Yes/ No	Yes/ No	Yes/ No	Yes/ No	Yes/ No	Yes/ No	Yes/ No
Individual Albums vs. Series:	10 Minimum	10 Minimum	10 Minimum	10 Minimum	Series Only	Individual Albums Available	Individual Albums Available	Individual Albums Available	Individual Albums Available	Individual Albums Available	Series Only	Individual Albums Available	Individual Albums Available	Individual Albums Available
Addition Policy Available Return:	Yes/ 30 Days	Yes/ 30 Days	Yes/ 30 Days	Yes/ 30 Days	No	No	Yes/ 30 Days	No/ 10 Days	Yes/ 45 Days	Yes/ 15 Days	—	No/ 10 Days	Yes/ 10 Days	No
Needle Drop Fee vs. Per Minute Used Fee:	$50 to $250 for Needle Drop	$50 to $250 for Needle Drop	$50 to $250 for Needle Drop	$50 to $250 for Needle Drop	Purchase of Albums Clears All Fees	Buy Out/ $89 per Album or $449 for 8	$50 per Needle Drop	Buy Out/ $175 per Album	Per Minute Used	$40 to $90 for Needle Drop Fee	$45 per Needle Drop	Buy Out/ Purchase Price	$40 per Needle Drop or $175 for 30 Minutes	Buy Out/ $100 per Album

Yearly License Available/ Fee:	Negotiable/ $10 per Album	Negotiable/ $10 per Album	Negotiable/ $10 per Album	Negotiable/ $10 per Album	Negotiable/ $10 per Album	Buy Out/ $89 per Album or $449 for 8	On Request	—	$2800/ Year License	$1350/ Year Buy Out	Buy Out Available	—	$1800/ Year (Broadcast)	—
Different Fee for Broadcast, Slide-film Non-broadcast Video, etc.:	Yes	Yes	Yes	Yes	Yes	No	Yes	No	No	Yes	—	No	Yes	No
Availability of Cues in Extended Versions and Tags/Average Length:	Extended: Yes; 1:00, Yes; :30, Yes; :10, Yes; Average: 2:00 to 3:00	Extended: Yes; 1:00, Yes; :30, Yes; :10, Yes; Average: 2:00 to 3:00	Extended: Yes; 1:00, Yes; :30, Yes; :10, Yes; Average: 2:00 to 3:00	Extended: Yes; 1:00, Yes; :30, Yes; :10, Yes; Average: 2:00 to 3:00	Average: :10 to 2:30	1:00, Yes; :30, Yes; Average:	Extended: Yes; 1:00, Yes; :30, Yes; :10, Yes; Average: 1:00 to 3:00	1:00, Yes; :30, Yes; :10, Yes; Average: 2:00	Extended: Yes; 1:00, Yes; :30, Yes; :10, Yes; Average: :29 to :59	Extended: Yes; 1:00, Yes; :30, Yes	Extended: Yes; 1:00, Yes; :30, Yes; :10, Yes; Average: 2:30	1:00, Yes; :30, Yes; Average: 2:00 to 4:00	Extended: Yes; 1:00, Yes; :30, Yes; :10, Yes; Average: 2:00 to 3:00	—
Rhythm Tracks/ Percent Available:	Yes/ 20%	Yes/ 20%	Yes/ 20%	Yes/ 20%	—	No	Yes/ 2	Yes/ 30%	Yes/ 100%	In Development	—	No	Yes/ 10%	—
Sound Effects Available	No	No	No	No	Yes	In Development	Yes	No	Yes	Yes (Football Only)	Yes (Science Fiction)	Yes	Yes	No
Special Services/ Additional Comments:	Music Scoring, Transfer and Editing	Music Scoring, Transfer and Editing	Music Scoring, Transfer and Editing	Music Scoring, Transfer and Editing	—	Custom Scoring, Narration and Track Building	—	Custom Music and Jingle Production	Custom Music Production	—	Original Music and "Music Selector"™ Software	—	Original Music	Custom Scoring/ Synthesizer Music Available

the theme song from the 'Sports Extra' show?" In fact, the NBC network promo department is using several Network cues for the trailers for the movies of the week, making it more difficult to find cues that haven't been heard before. The Network library is very versatile due to its design. Most of the pieces are built around a main theme 2 to 3 minutes in length, followed by versions lasting 60, 30, and 10 seconds, followed by a rhythm-track-only version that is often ideal for background under narration or dialog. Although several other libraries have certain albums employing this format, Network is the only library to present virtually all of its selections this way.

Of all the libraries available, KPM, Bruton, and Valentino are the most respected in terms of versatility, selection, and hi-fi sound recordings. The Valentino library, one of the oldest (if not *the* oldest) music library, is recorded primarily in the New York City area and is composed by many different artists. Bruton and KPM are both recorded in London and distributed by Associated Production Music (Los Angeles and New York). These three libraries are so extensive that virtually any type of music cue can be found. Both offer search and audition services.

Typically a production company or sweetening house has one or two complete libraries in addition to several albums from many other libraries. This is because one or two complete libraries can't always fill the bill for versatility that is required for all types of productions. Keeping track of one's library can be a difficult task, especially if albums are being sent on a weekly or monthly basis. Soper's Music-Selector software program can certainly help this effort, since it has room in its data base for non-Soper selections as well. Another method for keeping track of a library is the old standby three-ring binder, such as Network provides when the library is originally purchased. Updates are provided with each new album, when it is released. The pages contain all of the information for the album, plus space to write comments such as "bright, melodic piece featuring woodwinds and brass," or "used :60 on Robot Systems opening montage."

You can easily make your own library reference by customizing a page to fit your own requirements (see Fig. 9-2). Filling out the pages each time you get a new album and each time you use a given cue will not only let you familiarize yourself with your library, but will also help you keep better records of usage.

USING ORIGINAL MUSIC

Original music offers the video producer the most flexibility

Volume 9
Industrial

Record Side A

9-A2045	Achievement	1:59
9-A20456	Achievement	:59
9-A20453	Achievement	:29
9-A2045T	Achievement	:14
9-A2045R	Achievement	1:59

9-A2038	Evolution	2:50
9-A20386	Evolution	:59
9-A20383	Evolution	:29
9-A2038T	Evolution	:08
9-A2038R	Evolution	1:50

9-A2051	High Combustion	2:38
9-A20516	High Combustion	:59
9-A20513	High Combustion	:29
9-A2051T	High Combustion	:08
9-A2051R	High Combustion	2:02

Record Side B

9-B2005	Intrigue	4:19
9-B20056	Intrigue	:59
9-B20053	Intrigue	:29
9-B2005T	Intrigue	:09
9-B2005R	Intrigue	1:31

9-B2049	New Horizons	2:24
9-B20496	New Horizons	:59
9-B20493	New Horizons	:29
9-B2049T	New Horizons	:10
9-B2049R	New Horizons	1:36

9-B2034	Barren Journey	3:04
9-B20346	Barren Journey	:59
9-B20343	Barren Journey	:29
9-B2034T	Barren Journey	:15
9-B2034R	Barren Journey	2:09

Notes

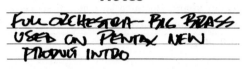

FULL ORCHESTRA - BIG BRASS USED ON PENTAX NEW PRODUCT INTRO

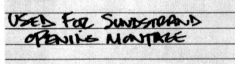

USED FOR SUNDSTRAND OPENING MONTAGE

USED FOR BILL CROUCH HONDA TV SPOTS

GOOD MONTAGE PIECE!

Fig. 9-2. Keeping notes of your music library, listing your impressions and what cues were used for which programs, creates a valuable reference.

and potential impact for the sound track. The disadvantages of original music are the price and turnaround time. However, the turnaround time need not be a factor at all, given proper planning. The purpose of this section is to make you aware of the planning, scheduling, communication, and pricing of original music. We will also discuss how to get what you need from an original sound track and how to communicate with the composer. Many times an original sound track may cost less than you think. With the advent of synthesizers, the cost of "electronic" sound tracks has come down in recent years. Because an original score is customized to exactly what you need, it can be highly effective in increasing the impact of a program.

Selecting a Composer

The first step in planning an original music score is to select a composer with whom to work. This should be done in much the same way you would select any other member of your production team. Talk with the composer and see if you feel comfortable working with him. Consider past experience and listen to a demo tape or other samples of work. Do not be afraid to ask questions. Talk with the composer about how he or she likes to work and on what kind of schedule.

Most composers of music for media are also the producers of the music in the recording studio. They should be able to handle all phases of the music composing, arranging, producing, recording, and delivery of the master tapes in the required format. This may vary slightly among composers, depending on the composer and the needs of the client, and may not be true of all composers for large-scale Hollywood film productions. For the purpose of this book, we will assume that the composer will provide all of the functions listed above. Of course, prices and rates need to be discussed as well. If you have not worked with a composer before, it is best to talk with a few of them before you decide.

Communication

The best thing you can do to assure success with original music is to communicate with the composer. This has to start with the goals of your program and what type of audience will be viewing it. But the communication needs to continue. You need to talk about budgets, schedules, your musical likes and dislikes, and in what type of format you need the music track. The fact that some of these items might change throughout production should be communicated as well.

This communication must be two-way. You need to make sure that the composer communicates with you about things he or she may feel uncomfortable with. It is the responsibility of the composer to let you know when your requests may be unreasonable or not practical. Also, the composer needs your honest opinions concerning the music. It is all right if you do not feel comfortable talking in musical terms. If you think you know what you want musically, however, it is a good idea to find some similar music to play for the composer. This will better communicate your ideas. Most composers are independent or work for smaller production companies. Therefore, any scheduling or pricing changes can be crucial. Even if there is a possibility of a change in these areas, it is best to communicate that and work out a contingency plan, should it become necessary.

It is best to bring in the composer right at the start of the production. Tell him what your plans are so he can work out his schedule—even if that means you might not need to talk with him for another month or two, which may be the case if the music is scored to the picture. If the picture is to be edited to the sound track, then the composer may start work right away. Composers of music for the visual medium are used to scoring to picture or storyboard. If scoring to a storyboard, it stands to reason that the more complete the storyboard, the tighter the sound track can be.

Once a storyboard or edited tape is ready, a new phase of communication must take place. This involves the information needed by the composer to write the music. If the music has not been spotted, now is the time. If you have already decided where music is to be used, then you should review each section with the composer and tell him what you need or want in each scene. Do not be afraid to ask the composer for ideas as well. You need to discuss with the composer the timing, moods, and transitions for each section requiring music. After this is done, the composer needs a copy of the video tape or storyboard for scoring. If scoring to picture, the video tape should have SMPTE time code window burned in. This is a great timesaver for you and the composer. Rough edits may be fine to work from as long as the timing information is accurate or can be otherwise communicated accurately.

Using Demos

It is always a good idea for the composer to supply you with a simple demo tape of some of the musical themes he is developing for you. Normally, this would be done simply, usually on a piano or synthesizer. The purpose is not to present a finished product, but to assist in the communication process between you and the composer, most composers can tell quite a bit from your reaction to a demo tape. Sometimes, however, it can be difficult to evaluate a demo tape. It is not much different from visualizing a finished program from a rough storyboard, so try to keep that in mind when working with demo tapes. Also, the composer may be able to play other material for you which will be more like the finished product, but with different themes. Here again, the bottom line is to keep the lines of communication open. Do not be afraid to use examples. In this way both you and the composer can be assured that what you want from the sound track is what you will get. Sometimes there might not be time for a demo tape, but if it is the first time you have worked with a particular composer, it is a very good idea.

Using Click Tracks

Sometimes you need tightly synchronized visual and audio, but for many considerations you have to have the music scored to picture. It is not unusual at all to have some scenes or sections which require the visuals to be edited to a musical beat. One way to handle this situation successfully is to decide, with or without the composer, what speed or tempo these beats or edit points need to be. Before editing begins, put down an audio click track on your EM; It is easiest for editing if the time between clicks is evenly divided by an integer number of video frames. Then, when making a copy of the videotape for the composer, either put the click track on for a reference or let the composer know how many frames there are between edits. Of course, this works best when the beat is steady for the length of the desired effect.

Sound Effects with Original Music

In planning an original music score, it is a good idea to look at your sound effects requirements at the same time. Many times the sound track can be enhanced by including some of those sound effects in the score. It can really make a cohesive sound track. Even if the sound effects are not in the score, it is still best for the composer to know where and what they are so he can write around them.

Licensing and Copyrights

There are many ways that licensing and copyrights can be handled with respect to original music for media. There are no standard agreements among composers on this topic. In general, however, the composer will want to keep the music copyright to himself. A buy-out of the music copyright is almost always negotiable for

174

an extra fee. This is just the music copyright or circle-c (©). The client always owns the circle-p (℗) copyright, which is the right to the master tape. That tape or copy of the tape should never be used without the permission and knowledge of the client. The composer should have the right to make copies for demonstration purposes only. Another way to think of this is that there is a "production fee" and a "creative fee." If you pay just the production fee, then you do not own the music copyright.

The composer will then license to the client the use of the music for the duration of what is needed. This could be for a week or forever. It usually involves a guarantee that the composer will not use that same melody in the same or similar market area for the agreed-upon time. All of these items are negotiable and should be discussed. However, they should not be a problem as long as there is good communication and documentation rights up front.

Costs

The cost of original music can vary widely. It is influenced by who the composer is, what the timetable is, what the instrumentation will be, whether it is scored to picture or not, how many musical "hits" there are, how much music is needed, and in what part of the country or world it is recorded. Listed in Table 9-2 are some price ranges that you can expect to pay for original music per finished minute. Generally, this would be for a minimum of 5 minutes of music. These prices include planning, composing, hiring musicians, booking studio time, and providing supplies for a finished music track. They do not necessarily include a completely sweetened audio track or a buy-out of the music copyright.

Although Table 9-2 shows a somewhat wide range, it gives you a good idea. If vocalists are used or there are other special considerations, the price could increase. If a number of projects are done together, however, it may be possible to get the price somewhat lower. Also, if there are some sections of music that are

Table 9-2. Typical Costs for Original Music.

Full Orchestra	$750 - $1500 per finished minute
Augmented Rhythm Section	$500 - $1000 per finished minute
This is a standard rhythm	
section plus strings, brass	
woodwinds, or heavy synthesizer	
Rhythm Section	$300 - $700 per finished minute
Includes keyboards, bass,	
drums, and guitar	
Synthesizer Only	$250 - $500 per finished minute

lightly scored—that is, with just a few instruments like piano and flute—that can keep the price down. Of course, every situation is different concerning original music, just as it is for original video.

Original Music in a Series

If you are producing a series of programs, whether it be for network, cable, educational, training, or any other use, it is possible to have original music throughout for a very reasonable cost. You can have a composer write a theme which would be common for the entire series. Then you can have a number of different variations of the theme recorded in different musical styles, each 2 to 3 minutes in length; these selections can be used as library selections throughout the series. But unlike conventional library music, all of the music for the series would tie together and have a common theme. This can really help to customize the music tracks at a much lower cost. I have done this a number of times for PBS and other series. The total cost for music may not be much different than if the producers had paid for needle drops for a 13-week series—yet they had their own theme and customized music. This is something to strongly consider for these types of situations.

THE BEST OF BOTH WORLDS

As mentioned earlier, it is possible to use both library and original music in the same program. In this way you can benefit from what both have to offer: the customizing of the original music and the cost savings of the library music. With this cost saving you may just be able to afford some original music, or you may be able to have your original music be a larger production than you could have afforded otherwise. If you decide to do this, it is best to pick out the library music with the composer, selecting it before the original music is written. Although this may not always be possible, it is a good idea if you can. In this way the composer can write their music so that it fits together well with the library music. This is even more important if the original music and library music will be adjacent in the program. The entire music track will flow better when the music can be written around the library music.

SUMMARY

As you can see, music plays a very important role in most programs. The more effectively you learn to use it to your benefit, the stronger your programs will be. Do not be afraid to experiment and try new things with your music tracks. Although it is true that a great music track will not save an otherwise terrible program, it can make a tremendous difference in how your audience responds. Learn to listen to and evaluate other programs, television and movies, to help you gain a greater understanding about how music does and does not work for you. You may be pleasantly surprised at the results.

Chapter 10

Facilities Considerations

---

sweet • en • ing bay \ 'swēt-ən-iŋ 'bā \ *n* a specially
configured room for making and improving sound tracks
for video programs

This chapter will introduce you to some of the considerations involved in building a sweetening bay or converting a video editing
bay for both editing and audio sweetening. This chapter is not intended to be a guide to acoustical design, but rather a point of
reference for what you need to consider—short of the best and most
expensive alternative: hiring an acoustical designer to design your
bay.

THE SWEETENING BAY

We will discuss the bay from two aspects, the audio/video
equipment complement and some basic acoustical considerations.
We will assume the bay is a combination video editing and audio
sweetening bay, since this will be typical of most smaller-scale environments (Fig. 10-1). Such a bay will also typically edit on 3/4"
video tape or edit interformat from 3/4" to 1". Typical 1"-to-1"
editing bays have too much equipment that would be tied up unnecessarily, or put out of service, to warrant adding sweetening
equipment. Under most circumstances, facilities with 1"-to-1"

Fig. 10-1. Hybrid sweetening bays (those used for both video tape editing and audio sweetening) tend to be occasionally cluttered as special projects necessitate bringing in other equipment. In this example, a Sony SMC-70G computer and a Cipher Digital Shadow are implemented for synchronization capability not available with the CMX Edge.

editing would find it economically advantageous to build a second bay, dedicated to sweetening but sharing VTRs with the edit bay.

From an equipment standpoint, the bay obviously must be configured with the necessary equipment to accomplish both video editing or machine control and synchronized audio sweetening. Consideration must be given to the personnel requirements of how the bay will be operated. Will one person accomplish all of the chores, or will the tasks be divided? For example, one individual could operate the video equipment and elements, while another person takes care of the audio equipment and elements. We at VCG have found the two-person complement to be most productive; otherwise, the task of operating all of the equipment *plus* paying careful attention to the sound becomes a burdensome task.

If you should decide to configure the bay for single-person operation, the controls for all of the equipment must be within reach of that one person (Fig. 10-2). This means that the video edit controller or synchronizer must be positioned to one side of the mixing console, and either the multitrack machine or its remote control unit must be positioned on the other side. Although the transport

179

Fig. 10-2. If the bay is designed for single-person operation, then all machine control functions, as well as track assignment capability, must be within the reach of the person operating the mixing console. In this case, Milt Hubatka can control the remote machines with the CMX Edge, make the TASCAM 58 channel assignments using that machine's own RC-51 remote control, and run the Otari 1/2" 4-track to his right directly.

control (play, record, search, and rewind) is controlled automatically by the edit controller or synchronizer (either chase-mode or intelligent controller), the track selection functions on the multitrack must be controlled either from its front panel or via its remote control.

The tasks of changing source tapes, cuing records, etc., must still be dealt with, however, and on occasion this may require more than one person during a sweetening session. Mixing can be done by one person, though, if the bay is properly configured.

If you design the bay for two-person operation, things become a bit simpler, and certainly less confusing (Fig. 10-3). Additionally, the sweetening process might not be such a lonely task and be more open to creative collaboration. The tasks can be easily divided between two people, letting one person be responsible for the control functions, while the other person is responsible for the audio.

Ideally, the mixing console should be set evenly between the two monitor speakers to facilitate the mixing of stereo, if that is a common occurrence (Fig. 10-4). Otherwise, the mixing console

Fig. 10-3. The authors' preferred setup is for two-person operation. Typically, Fred Hull operates the CMX Edge and Milt Hubatka sits behind the mixing console. In this manner, the sweetening session is much more of a collaborative process.

Fig. 10-4. Placing the mixing console between both speakers is essential when mixing stereo sound tracks.

should have cables long enough to be moved to the center when necessary. Counter space and work space always seem to be at a premium in an editing suite with edit controllers, video switchers, and the like; with the addition of synchronizer controllers and mixing consoles, the space becomes even more precious because there must still be room for a producer or director to work with a script and other production materials.

Some design consideration and planning must be given to the wiring of the sweetening bay. First, all the audio equipment can be hard-wired together, or an audio patch bay can be installed. Each method has its own advantages. Hard-wiring takes less planning and is faster to install and implement, but a patch bay brings all of the audio connections from the mixing board, tape machines, and other outboard equipment to a common point. Then, all connections are made with the use of short patch cables.

The most common setups are normalled, or hard-wired through the patch bay. In this way, a minimum of patching is needed for most routine setups. This is much more flexible and lets the operator connect any piece of equipment to any other piece of equipment, easily and without tripping over cables. It also allows for easy and painless expansion and/or interchanging of equipment. Consider your particular situation and pick the method that is best for you.

During the wiring of the audio equipment, special care must be taken with balanced and unbalanced connections, as discussed in Chapter 3. You must also pay special attention to the *grounding* situation with each piece of equipment. "Ground loops" are the single biggest hassle in putting together different pieces of audio equipment. If this is something you are not comfortable with, it is best to get some professional audio assistance at this stage of the game.

In designing your sweetening/edit bay, make sure to plan enough space for extra people; you also need some storage space for audio and video tapes that are related to any particular program. In addition, you need space for music and sound effects libraries, scripts, notes, and whatever else may be needed for your program—not the least of which is a place to put your cup of coffee without spilling it all over the mixing board.

ACOUSTIC CONSIDERATIONS

One of the primary considerations in designing an audio sweetening bay has to be that of acoustics. Many excellent books are available on the subject of studio and control room acoustics, so we will not attempt to duplicate that information. What we want to achieve in the sweetening bay is an acoustical environment that is as *flat* as possible (Fig. 10-5). In other words, we want to hear what is really there. We do not want some frequencies to be louder or softer than other frequencies. We also want the room to *reference* properly. That is, we want what sounds good in our sweetening bay to sound good in any other environment in which it is played.

If you are remodeling or building a new facility, then you have some options available in your construction. It is best to not have parallel walls in your listening environment. This prevents standing waves, thereby helping keep the room flat. You can also have alcoves built for equipment racks, storage, etc. If you can, it is best to have a consultant assist with the design of your facility if you are building or remodeling. If you elect to modify an existing room, then consider using a soft foam acoustical treatment such as Sonex on any parallel walls. The rear wall can be a special problem, especially if the room is not very deep. Sound reflections from the rear wall can affect the sound that you hear from the speaker, causing constructive and destructive interference. This does not let you hear just what is coming out of the speakers. Sonex will help here as well.

A very important consideration in how your sweetening bay will sound is the speaker system through which you listen. When selecting monitor speakers, pay special attention to how they are designed to be used. All quality monitor speakers are designed with a specific purpose in mind. Some are designed to be set flush against a wall, while others are designed to be placed a foot or two away from any surfaces. Yet other speakers are designed to be mounted in a wall so that the speaker itself is flush with the wall. You need to figure out what is best for your situation, and then find speakers that meet your requirements. Do not buy speakers simply because you can get a good price when you are using the speakers to reference all of your audio decisions.

Fig. 10-5. A graphic equalizer with a spectrum display is ideal for setting up a bay and making it acoustically "flat," so no one frequency is louder or softer than any other. Once the room is set up, the controls of the equalizer are not touched (courtesy TASCAM).

If you have a relatively small room, or if there is not much you can do to the room to make it a good listening environment, then the best solution is to use speakers that are designed for *near-field* monitoring. This means that they are designed to work well when the listener is close to them. The philosophy here is that the closer your ear is to the speaker, the less the room will affect what you hear.

Rooms can be made flat by equalizing the room with a real-time analyzer. Pink noise is fed to the monitor speakers, and a microphone is placed where the mixer is most likely to sit. The microphone output is fed into the real-time analyzer, which tells what frequencies are present and in what amounts. With a 1/3 octave equalizer it is possible to compensate for the speakers and the room, so as to make the room flat. This requires an equalizer for each speaker. Once this is done, the equalizers should be closed up and left alone.

All of this will help us achieve a room that will reference well. A flat room does not guarantee this, but it is a large step in the right direction. No two rooms or environments will sound exactly the same. You need to do some mixes in your room and listen to them in a few different places. Also listen to some other tapes or records you are familiar with in your sweetening bay. It will help you to see rather quickly how close you are. However, it will still take a little while for you to feel comfortable and confident with your sweetening bay. If your room is not playing enough bass, then in other place your mixes will sound bassy, because you have over-compensated from the lack of bass in your sweetening bay. You just need to pay attention to this and learn to work with it. As you progress you may make some changes in your room to help you feel more confident. There is fairly low-cost equipment available to help you in making your bay as flat as possible. Do not make drastic changes all at once, or you will lose your perspective. This is especially true if you are continuing to mix in your bay on a daily basis.

THE IDEAL HYBRID BAY

The sweetening bay we have at the Visual Communications Group, Inc., is far from perfect and not nearly state-of-the-art, but for all intents and purposes it is highly functional. We did not have a large budget when we decided to enter the field of audio sweetening, and have in effect "bootstrapped" the operation, adding equipment little by little as the need arose or finances allowed.

Since VCG is a production entity and not a postproduction facility, our bay is a hybrid sweetening bay, part video edit bay and part audio sweetening bay. We have a computerized video tape editor (a CMX Edge), which controls VTRs and an ATR through a home-brew interface (Fig. 10-6). Since it is more convenient for us to control all machines through one computer, we decided to use the Edge (as opposed to a synchronizer), for this function. We have experimented with both the Cipher Digital Shadow and Softouch, as well as the Adams-Smith 2600 system, and found both to be exceptional devices. CMX gave us little support in building the direct machine control interface for the Edge, citing a synchronizer as the best solution short of buying a 3400X with an intelligent interface—which of course wouldn't interface with low-cost multitracks such as the TASCAM 58.

Considering costs and keeping with "small-scale" productions in mind, in our estimation the "ideal" hybrid video/audio bay would use an intelligent synchronizer such as the Adams-Smith 2600 or Cipher Digital Shadow /Softpad system to control the machines (Fig. 10-7). Devices such as these provide all the necessary functions, including record punch-in and punch-out, through one

Fig. 10-6. This is a home-brew machine control interface designed by Fred Hull that allows the CMX Edge to control the TASCAM 58 8-track ATR. Although CMX offers intelligent interfaces for some ATRs, they are only available for CMX large-scale systems. It is desirable to have one device control both video editing machines and machines for audio sweetening, but it is not essential.

keyboard, under the control of one device. Although this setup would not edit video tape, the video editor could be configured easily into the bay when the primary function is video tape editing.

The "ideal" hybrid bay can have either a 3/4"-to-3/4" or a 3/4"-to-1" interformat video complement, depending on the type of work and the available budget. Having a 1" machine, however, offers industry compatibility, as does having a 1/2" 4-track ATR.

A 1/2" 8-track ATR would be our choice for the master multitrack, mostly due to good price/performance ratios. Although 16 tracks would be nice, under most conditions 8 tracks are adequate. Either the TASCAM 58 or the Otari 5050 Mark III 8-track is ideally suited to these applications. The cost of a 16-track recorder, both to purchase and to keep supplied in 1" tape, in our opinion transcends small-scale productions. Fostex does manufacture a 1/2" 16-track ATR, but we have no experience with it.

Having an additional multitrack ATR is very useful, although not essential, unless you must have compatibility with the outside world. Often during a track-building session you will encounter a situation when you will want to build a presence loop or some other element on a multitrack machine, then mix it and lay it over to the master multitrack. Unless you take down your master reel from

Fig. 10-7. Another small-scale audio sweetening bay called The Audio Post (Canoga Park, California) utilizes an Otari Mark III 8-track ATR and a Cipher Digital synchronizer.

Fig. 10-8. A high-quality audio cassette machine is very useful in a sweetening bay; it is inexpensive to purchase and offers the capability for fast cuing of sound effects, as well as background presence (courtesy TASCAM).

your 8-track, build the sequence, and mix it to another medium (such as 1/4" 2-track, audio or video cassette) you will require another machine. A 1/2" 4-track is closest to the ideal candidate for the extra multitrack. Of course, every sweetening bay also must have a 1/4" 2-track for narration, music, editing, loops, etc. Although not essential, an audio cassette machine is also very nice to have (Fig. 10-8).

One can spend a great deal of money—and perhaps kill an entire budget—on a sophisticated mixing console, when there are many available in the $3000 to $5000 range that provide all the necessary functions. The main criterion is the number of inputs and the number of buses, or outputs. Obviously the console should have as many buses as tracks of your multitrack ATR. Other considerations for mixing consoles include the amount of equalization and the number of auxiliary buses. We have found the TASCAM M-50 to be more than adequate and very cost-effective.

Outboard equipment is always desirable but is often left out, along with the last elements on the "wish list." Equalization is nice to have, but it tends to duplicate to a degree what is available in the console itself. A good parametric equalizer, with both high- and low-pass filters, is an invaluable tool. If we had to choose only one piece of outboard equipment—considering EQ, noise reduction, digital reverb, etc.—we should choose a compressor/limiter. A compressor/limiter is one of the most useful devices available for audio sweetening, and is duplicated nowhere else in the system. We en-

Fig. 10-9. The sweetening bay at The Visual Communications Group, Inc. (Boulder, Colorado) is small but dynamic, in that it can easily be reconfigured for a variety of tasks. Since this photo was taken, the bay has been converted from an off-line video/sweetening bay to a 3/4"-to-1" interformat edit bay with synchronized 8-track sweetening, all under CMX Edge control.

counter dialog, narration, music, or effects that have tremendous dynamic range more often than anything else, and need help in keeping them under control.

Noise reduction is very useful, but might be considered overkill when budgets are tight. If the bulk of work coming out of the bay is played in large rooms with great speakers and sound systems, dbx or Dolby might be highly desirable. On the other hand, if the majority of the work is being distributed on VHS, to be played through TV speakers, noise reduction may or may not make any difference in the end product.

The more esoteric equipment, such as aural exciters, compellors, digital delays, noise gates, etc., are more readily found in high-end sweetening bays, of Hollywood scale, than in bays designed for the sweetening of small-scale productions (Fig. 10-9).

Chapter 11

The Future
of Small-Scale
Audio Sweetening

dig • i • tal \ ' dij-ət-əl \ **1** : *adj* of or relating to a way of storing and representing as binary numbers information such as audio elements **2** : *n* a kind of technology that eliminates generational losses inherent in analog storage systems such as magnetic tape

Technology has a played an all-important role in bringing high-quality audio sweetening capabilities within the economic reach of producers of small-scale productions. This technology has been exemplified by low-cost, high-quality multitrack ATRs such as the TASCAM Model 58 and Otari 5050 series. Synchronizers such as the Cipher Digital Shadowpad or Adams-Smith 2600, which offer two-machine computer control, have given us all of the capability available only to major Hollywood facilities had to offer just a few years ago (Fig. 11-1).

Microprocessor technology has made an impact on our lives, the way we work (in terms of personal computers), and the way we edit video and sweeten audio. The computer-on-a-chip has made our VTRs and ATRs more intelligent and allows for the precise synchronization of both. Integrated circuit technology has made our audio systems quieter, yielding greater dynamic range. This trend will certainly continue, although we probably won't continue to see the tremendous price erosion that we have experienced in the past

Fig. 11-1. The microprocessor has made audio sweetening for small-scale productions achievable, due to the intelligence now available in computerized editors, synchronizers, and multitrack ATRs.

five years. The VTRs and multitrack ATRs probably have decreased in price about as much as possible, due to the tremendous number of mechanical elements necessary to make them functional.

In the next few years, however, we will probably see better price/performance ratios. More tracks will be crammed on smaller tape, as evidenced by the Fostex machines having 16 instead of the current 8 tracks on 1/2" audio tape. We will continue to see greater dynamic range and signal-to-noise ratios on multitrack equipment and consoles, as well as increased audio capabilities and improved specifications of video cassette machines. As evidenced by hi-fi Beta and VHS machines already available, the next generation of 3/4" cassette machines could conceivably have two audio channels with specs rivaling today's multitracks.

The trends in technology always seems to appear first in the high-end equipment used in recording studios or Hollywood-scale sweetening bays. That is where digital recording technology has made its mark. Digital technology is quieter and does not accumulate noise through generations of reproduction. Many major albums are being recorded on multitrack digital recorders today, but it will probably be 5 years or so before we see that technology filter down to the multitracks offered by firms such as TASCAM and Otari. Teac, the parent company that manufacturers TASCAM

190

professional products, has been manufacturing digital data recorders for many years and is in an excellent position to release the small scale digital multitrack ATR. According to Dave Oren, marketing manager for TASCAM professional products, "As soon as a standard of digital recording is adopted, digital recorders from TASCAM will soon be available."

The state-of-the-art recording technology for major record albums has become almost totally digital, going from digital mixing console to digital recording on multitrack tape and mixing to digital 2-track machines, followed by digital mastering to compact disks and final conversion to analog only when the signal reaches the amplifier in your living room.

Almost every element in high-end audio sweetening is still primarily analog, however, and we probably won't see (or hear) a change for 3 to 5 years, until major facilities such as Glen Glenn Sound amortize the cost of their current multitrack analog equipment, although Glen Glenn already has a Sony 24-track digital recorder (Fig. 11-2). But the real bottom line here is that making a transition to digital wouldn't add much, due to the general lack of quality in television and motion picture theater sound technology.

In 1984, however, Glen Glenn did produce a sound track for

Fig. 11-2. The sweetening bays at Glen Glenn Sound in Hollywood are capable of digital recording, although most of the work done there is still analog.

a program titled "Digital Dream," in which the entire process was digital. Starting in the field with modified Sony PCM F-1 portable recorders for all sync sound, the digital process was carried all the way through on their proprietary Digitrac system. All-digital audio postproduction will begin life with major motion pictures—once theater sound systems are converted to digital—but probably will not filter down to television for many years, except perhaps for MTV-type stereo distribution.

Another impact of digital technology is that of sound effects systems that store the effect "digitally" in computer memory; these allow manipulation of the effect in terms of altered speed and equalization through input from a computer keyboard. A system called ACCESS (for Automated Computer Controlled Editing Sound System) is an example of this technology, as is a system called ASP developed by Lucasfilm and used extensively for sound effects creation in *Indiana Jones and the Temple of Doom*. This system may at some point become commercially available, as is the Lucasfilm "EditDroid," codeveloped with Convergence Corporation. It is probably unlikely that such digital sound effects processing systems will become cost-effective enough to be part of the toolbox for producers of smaller-scale productions for many years.

Laser disk technology, however, will be seen in smaller-scale sweetening bays very soon. The technology is already available and is in the price bracket for our scale of sweetening. The main obstacle now is simply the availability of the program material on the medium. Screen Sound Services president, Steve Waldman, a pioneer in high-technology audio for video and film, introduced a Laser disk sound effects system based on the Sony SMC-70 and Sony Laser disk system at the 1984 National Association of Broadcasters convention. By typing a sound effects cue ID into the keyboard, the disk will cue and play the effect automatically. This system is available now, but currently you must have your own effects library mastered to the disk at a cost of about $300 each.

The other medium making an impact on small-scale productions is the compact disk, operating under the control of a computer. Harn Soper of Soper Sound has recently released an enhanced version of the Soper Music-Selector database management system (discussed in Chapter 9), which will interface directly with the Matsushita compact disk player; the entire Soper Sound library will be available on CD. You can run the Music-Selector program on an IBM PC and type in some parameters for a cue, such as desired instrumentation, length, mood, etc.; the program will search the library, instruct the operator to insert the appropriate compact disk, and then automatically seek the proper track and play the cue. After

Fig. 11-3. In the near future we will probably see an increase in performance of mixing consoles, in that they will be quieter, offer more capability in terms of features. Automated mixing consoles in the $5,000-to-$10,000 range should be plentiful by the end of the decade.

this preview, the cue can then be transferred to the multitrack during the appropriate stage in the sweetening process. Although we haven't heard of such a system currently in existence, the day should draw near when a complete sound effects library, such as Network's, will appear on computer-controlled compact disk. In fact, Network is planning on having both its sound effects and music library released on CD, under computer control, by early 1986.

Automated mixing consoles in the $5000 to $10,000 price range should also be available in 2 to 3 years, offering the ability to accomplish virtually flawless mixes (Fig. 11-3). Soon we will also see automated mixing consoles under control of video editors such as those now available from ISC (Interactive Systems Company), of Boulder, Colorado. The video edit controller (currently in the $20,000 to $30,000 price range) can interface to automated consoles, enabling the editor to place events in an edit decision list and to automate such functions under fader control.

Quieter, lower-cost mixing consoles, offering more busing and more internal EQ capability, are on the near-term horizon and will soon be seen from manufacturers such as TASCAM and Yamaha.

Since mixing consoles are totally electronic, having virtually no expensive mechanical elements such as tape transports, the progressive improvement in price/performance ratios will continue to have a positive effect on these hardware elements in the audio sweetening chain. While we may not see any price decrease in multitrack recorders, we will see electronic performance increases in both recorders and consoles in terms of audio *quality*, with machines that are quieter and have better signal-to-noise ratios and improved dynamic range.

Double-system recording capability with cassette machines will soon be making its way into industrial-scale production. The audio cassette technology of 1985, utilizing metal tape and Dolby C, far surpasses the frequency response and signal-to-noise ratios of both 3/4" video cassette and component video such as M-Format and Sony's BetaCam. TASCAM's Porta-One 4-track cassette (Fig. 11-4) and the Sony TCD-6C both offer high-quality audio and the capability of time coding the tracks for later "bumping" to another

Fig. 11-4. Trends toward higher-density, higher-performance recording formats are exemplified by TASCAM's "Porta-One," a 4-track cassette recorder with built-in dbx noise reduction and mixing console, as well as sync recording capability and punch-in.

Fig. 11-5. Regardless of the advances in equipment, audiences will continue to demand better and better sound tracks. Composer/producer/engineer Rich Sanders mixes an original musical score for a recent production by the authors.

medium that can be controlled by a synchronizer, such as 1/2" or 1/4" tape.

In the next few years we may see a decrease in prices of outboard equipment, such as noise reduction, equalization, digital reverb, and the like. As more and more electronic circuitry is reduced to LSI or "chip" technology, these devices will become less complicated and hence less expensive to manufacture. It is unlikely that any further price reduction will be seen in multitrack recorders, since the production volume is relatively low (compared to consumer electronic items such as video cassette recorders), combined with the fact that ATRs are mostly mechanical.

With stereo television and hi-fi video cassettes leading the revolution, we will continue to experience the demand for higher and higher quality in the audio tracks accompanying video programs (Fig. 11-5). MTV has helped to generate a tremendous awareness of both stereo and high-quality and audio tracks, and we are already seeing network TV programs released in stereo.

Producers will not be able to "get away" with producing programs with mediocre sound tracks, because sophisticated audiences won't tolerate it. This book has attempted to address the basic concepts applicable to audio sweetening and to provide the necessary background in hardware and technique to give anyone the ability to begin to create more pleasing sound tracks for video programs. The expression "chops don't come in a box" should be mentioned again, for we must reiterate . . . practice and you will perfect the skills that are necessary to create great sound tracks.

Appendix A

Sweetening Hardware Sources

ADM Technology
1626 E. Beaver Rd.
Troy, MI 48084
(313) 524-2100

Adams-Smith
34 Tower St.
Hudson, MA 01749
(617) 562-3801

Amek Console (USA)
10815 Burbank Blvd.
North Hollywood, CA 91601
(818) 508-9788

Ampex Corp.
401 Broadway
Redwood City, CA 94063
(415) 367-2011

Ampro/Scully
2360 Industrial La.
Broomfield, CO 80020
(303) 465-4141

Arrakis
309 Commerce Dr.
Fort Collins, CO 80524
(303) 224-2248

Audio & Design/Calrec
Box 786
Bremerton, WA 98310
(206) 275-5009

Audio Kinetics, Inc.
4721 Laurel Canyon Blvd., Ste. 209
North Hollywood, CA 91607
(818) 980-5717

Audio Processing Systems
90 Oak St.
Newton Upper Falls, MA 02614
(617) 965-1200

Audio-Technica U.S., Inc.
1221 Commerce Dr.
Stow, OH 44224
(216) 686-2600

Auditronics
3750 Old Getwell Rd.
Memphis, TN 38118
(901) 362-1350

Autogram Corp.
631 J. Pl.
Plano, TX 75074
(214) 424-8585

BTX/Cipher Digital
10 Kearney Rd.
Needham, MA 02194
(617) 449-7546

Broadcast Audio Corp.
11306 Sunco Dr.
Rancho Cordova, CA 95670
(916) 635-1048

Broadcast Electronics
4100 N. 24 St.
Quincy, IL 62305
(217) 224-9600

CMX Orrox
3303 Scott Blvd.
Santa Clara, CA 95050
(408) 988-2000

Comprehensive Video Supply
148 Veterans Dr.
Northvale, NJ 07647
(201) 767-7990

Crown International
1718 W. Mishawaka Rd.
Elkhart, IN 46517
(219) 294-5571

Datatronix
210 Reston Ave.
Reston, VA 22091
(703) 620-5300

Electro-Voice
600 Cecil St.
Buchanan, MI 49107
(616) 695-6831

Fostex Corp. of America
15431 Blackburn Ave.
Norwalk, CA 90650
(213) 921-1112

Gotham Audio
741 Washington St.
New York, NY 10014
(212) 741-7411

Harris
Box 4290
Quincy, IL 62305
(217) 222-8200

Harrison Systems
Box 22964
Nashville, TN 37202
(615) 834-1184

Integrated Sound Systems
29-50 Northern Blvd.
Long Island City, NY 11101
(212) 729-8400

International Music Co./Studiomaster
1316 E. Lancaster
Fort Worth, TX 76102
(817) 336-5114

JBL/UREI
8500 Balboa Blvd.
Northridge, CA 91329
(818) 893-8411

Lexicon
60 Turner St.
Waltham, MA 02154
(617) 891-6790

Nagra Magnetic Recorders, Inc.
19 W. 44 St., Rm. 715
New York, NY 10036
(212) 840-0999
            or
1147 N. Vine St.
Hollywood, CA 90038
(213) 469-6391

Neotek
1154 W. Belmont Ave.
Chicago, IL 60657
(312) 929-6699

Rupert Neve
Berkshire Industrial Park
Bethel, CT 06801
(203) 744-6230

Orban Associates, Inc.
645 Bryant St.
San Francisco, CA 94107
(415) 957-1067

Otari Corp.
2 Davis Dr.
Belmont, CA 94002
(415) 592-8311

Pacific Recorders & Engineering
2070 Las Palmas Dr.
Carlsbad, CA 92008
(619) 438-3911

Panasonic/Ramsa
1 Panasonic Way
Secaucus, NJ 07094
(201) 348-7397

Quad Eight/Westrex
11929 Vose St.
North Hollywood, CA 91605
(818) 764-1516

Quantum Audio Labs
1905 Riverside Dr.
Glendale, CA 91201
(213) 841-0970

RTS Systems
1100 W. Chestnut St.
Burbank, CA 91506
(818) 843-7022

Screen Sound, Inc.
4721 Laurel Canyon Blvd.
North Hollywood, CA 91607
(818) 761-0323

Sennheiser Electronic Corp. (NY)
48 W. 38 St.
New York, NY 10018
(212) 239-0190

Shure Bros.
222 Hartrey Ave.
Evanston, IL 60204
(312) 866-2200

Solid State Logic
200 W. 57 St.
New York, NY 10019
(212) 315-1111

Sony Pro Audio/MCI
1 Sony Dr.
Park Ridge, NJ 07656
(201) 930-1000

Soundcraft Electronics
1517 20 St.
Santa Monica, CA 90404
(213) 453-4591

Spectra Sonics
3750 Airport Rd.
Ogden, UT 84405
(801) 392-7531

Studer Revox America
1425 Elm Hill Pike
Nashville, TN 37210
(615) 254-5651

Tannoy North America, Inc.
97 Victoria St.
North Kitchener, ONT
Canada N2H5C1
(519) 745-1158

Tascam/TEAC
7733 Telegraph Rd.
Montebello, CA 90640
(213) 726-0303

Technical Audio Devices (TAD)
Professional Products Div. of
Pioneer Electronics (USA), Inc.
5000 Airport Plaza Dr.
Long Beach, CA 90815
(213) 420-5700

Tel-Test
P.O. Box 1475
Gainesville, FL 32602
(904) 374-4503

Transit O Sound
728 Yosemite Dr.
Indianapolis, IN 46217
(317) 787-8491

Trident USA
280 Mill St. Ext.
Lancaster, MA 01523
(617) 365-2130

Ultra Audio Pixtec
Box 921
Beverly Hills, CA 90213
(213) 651-5563

Valley People, Inc.
P.O. Box 40306
2817 Erica Pl.
Nashville, TN 37204
(615) 383-4737

Ward-Beck Systems
841 Progress Ave.
Scarborough, ONT
Canada M1H2X4
(416) 438-6550

Yamaha International
6600 Orangethorpe Ave.
Buena Park, CA 90620
(714) 522-9011

Appendix B

Sweetening Software Sources

MUSIC LIBRARIES

Aircraft Music Library
77 North Washington Street
Boston, MA 02114
(800) 343-2514

Emil Asher Music
630 5th Avenue
New York, NY 10111
(212) 581-4504

Associated Production Music
6255 Sunset Blvd.
Hollywood, CA 90028
(213) 461-3211
             or
888 7th Avenue, 12th Floor
New York, NY 10106
(212) 977-5685

Bruton Music
c/o Associated Production Music
6255 Sunset Blvd.
Hollywood, CA 90028
(213) 461-3211
                    or
888 7th Avenue, 12th Floor
New York, NY 10106
(212) 977-5685

Capitol Production Music
1750 North Vine
Hollywood, CA 90028
(213) 461-2701

Chapel Music
c/o Musicues
1156 Avenue of the Americas
New York, NY 10036
(212) 757-3641

Comprehensive Video Supply Corporation
148 Veterans Drive
Northvale, NJ 07647
(201) 767-7990 or (800) 526-0242

Conroy & Themes International
c/o Associated Production Music
6255 Sunset Blvd.
Hollywood, CA 90028
(213) 461-3211
                    or
888 7th Avenue, 12th Floor
New York, NY 10106
(212) 977-5685

Creative Support Services or Repro-File
1950 Riverside Drive
Los Angeles, CA 90039
(213) 666-7968

DeWolfe Music Library, Inc.
25 West 45th Street
New York, NY 10036
(212) 382-0220

Films for the Humanities
P.O. Box 2053
or
743 Alexander Road
Princeton, NJ 08540
(609) 452-1128 or (800) 257-5126

KPM
c/o Associated Production Music
6255 Sunset Blvd.
Hollywood, CA 90028
(213) 461-3211
or
888 7th Avenue, 12th Floor
New York, NY 10106
(212) 977-5685

MusiCrafters
P.O. Box 1301
Doylestown, PA 18901
(215) 345-TUNE

Music Masters, Inc.
17 Ponca Trail
St. Louis, MO 63122
(314) 821-2741

Musicues
1156 Avenue of the Americas
New York, NY 10036
(212) 757-3641

Network Production Music, Inc.
4429 Morena Blvd.
San Diego, CA 92117
(619) 272-2011 or (800) 854-2075

NFL Films Music Library
330 Fellowship Road
Mt. Laurel, NJ 08054
(215) 925-6017 or (609) 778-1600

NLR (No License Required Music Library)
P.O. Box 290007
Ft. Lauderdale, FL 33329
(305) 581-9053

Omnimusic
52 Main Street
Port Washington, NY 11050
(516) 883-0121, Collect calls accepted

Regent Recorded Music, Inc.
7060 Hollywood Blvd., Suite 800
Los Angeles, CA 90028
(213) 461-9926

Repro-File or Creative Support Services
1950 Riverside Drive
Los Angeles, CA 90039
(213) 666-7968

Soper Sound Music Library
P.O. Box 498
Palo Alto, CA 94302
(415) 321-4022 or (800) 227-9980

Themes/ZM Squared
903 Edgewood Lane, P.O. Box C-30
Cinnaminson, NJ 08077
(609) 786-0612

TRF Music, Inc.
40 East 49th Street
New York, NY 10017
(212) 753-3234

Valentino Production Music Library
151 West 46th Street
New York, NY 10036
(212) 869-5210 or (800) 223-6278

Voyage Music Library
686 South Arroyo Parkway, Suite 106
Pasadena, CA 91105
(818) 795-6723 or (213) 795-6723

SOUND EFFECTS LIBRARIES

Bainbridge Entertainment Co., Inc.
P.O. Box 8248
Van Nuys, CA 91409-8248
(800) 621-8705

Network Production Music, Inc.
4429 Morena Blvd.
San Diego, CA 92117
(619) 272-2011 or (800) 854-2075

Production EFFX Library
c/o Toby's Tunes, Inc.
2325 Girard Ave. S.
Minneapolis, MN 55405
(612) 377-0690

Valentino Production Music Library
151 West 46th Street
New York, NY 10036
(212) 869-5210 or (800) 223-6278

ASSOCIATIONS

Production Music Library Association
40 East 49th Street, Suite 605
New York, NY 10017
(212) 832-1098

Glossary

access time—Time required to retrieve video information during editing or assembly.

automatic dialog replacement (ADR)—The process of replacing production dialog wherein talent views picture and listens to production audio track while reciting the dialog in sync. The non-automated method is termed "looping."

alligator tail—Swishing or whooshing sound artificially created to simulate clothing noise or rustle, often used to cover holes in the production track.

ambient sound—The natural sounds that are recorded at time of shooting.

ATR—Abbreviation for *audio tape recorder.*

audio cassette—Standard audio tape cassette used for consumer distribution of audio programming such as music albums and lectures; used in sweetening for sound effects, wild sounds, background presence, etc.

autoassemble—Automatic generation of an edited master video or audio tape in conformance with a stored edit decision list by a computerized video edit controller.

automated consoles—A mixing console used to mix or remix audio programming, capable of storing or remembering control settings such as fader levels or EQ setups, allowing the operator to automatically duplicate a mix with or without altering selected control settings.

auxiliary channel—Additional outputs from a mixing console, separate from the primary bus and monitor outputs. An aux channel allows a different mix to be sent to a different destination, e.g., a performer's cue or an effects processor.

auxiliary channel send controls—These controls allow varying levels of a single input channel to be fed to different auxiliary channels (e.g., echo or cue channels). Additional controls often allow the main fader and/or equalization to affect the auxiliary channel feed and allow panning between different sets of auxiliary channels. In sound reinforcement consoles these can be the main output channel feeds.

auxiliary returns—Additional inputs to a mixing console used to incorporate auxiliary sources or to reintroduce a processed signal from an outboard processor such as echo or reverb.

back-time—To calculate an edit in point by finding the out point and subtracting the duration of the edit.

balanced input—Processing mode for inputs in which the signals on the two input wires are isolated from system ground and one signal is effectively subtracted from the other, thus eliminating any noise or interference common to both wires. Different devices use either transformers or electronic differential amplifiers to perform this process.

bass trap—A mechanical construction installed in an acoustical environment to absorb bass tones, designed and placed to prevent the bass echos from contaminating the direct transmission of the sound.

boot (bootstrap)—A primitive program stored in a computer memory whose function is to load a more powerful operating program from a peripheral device.

bus—In a mixing console, a conceptual collector or summer of other signals. Input signals are mixed together into a bus circuit or signal line. The mixed signal travels from the bus to an output connector and other internal functions.

bus assignment controls—Used to assign inputs to buses in a multioutput console.

capstan—In an audio tape recorder, a motor-driven shaft or spindle used to drive a magnetic tape by pulling it at uniform speed.

capstan servo—An electronic circuit that controls capstan speed relative to a reference signal. The reference may be fixed for constant tape speed or varied to dynamically adjust the tape speed.

cathode ray tube (CRT)—The picture tube of a television monitor.

channel—A communication line; a pathway for electronic signals.

clap sticks—A pair of hinged sticks often attached to a chalkboard or slate. The sticks are clapped together in front of a camera while shooting film and recording audio, giving a reference point for synchronizing the audio to the film in postproduction.

communications facilities—In a mixing console, the provision to "talk back" to people in the studio through headphones; similar to an intercom or PA system.

console—A module or portion of a device externally accessible to an operator for display and control of information and device functions; often remote, as on a desktop.

crosstalk—Interference in an electronic signal from another signal caused by magnetic field overlaps in tape heads, leakage through circuits, or proximity of nonshielded wires.

cue—The operation through which a magnetic tape is stopped in a predeteremined position ahead of the edit in point.

cue—1. A segment or band (on a record) of music or sound effect. 2. A program feed to a performer for monitoring other performers, program status, etc.

cut—The instantaneous transition from one information source to another.

CPU—Central Processing Unit, the main brain of a computer.

data lines—Serial or parallel lines used exclusively for transfer or communication of data usually encoded in digital format, such as binary or ASCII.

dialog—The lines spoken by on-camera talent.

dissolve—An edit transition where one source of video or audio fades out while at the same time a new source fades in.

distortion—An alteration in the fundamental character of an electronic signal. In audio, a change in the essential frequency content of a sound caused by imperfect reproduction in an amplifier or a record/reproduction process.

drop frame—A convention for modifying the frame counting sequence of the time code such that the code difference between two program points exactly represents the actual clock time elapsed between the points.

dub/dupe—A video or audio tape duplicate. Dub is used to mean "copy" in both video and audio work. In film work, "dubbing" means integrating and mixing the audio units or tracks.

duration—The length of time (in hours, minutes, seconds, and frames) that a particular effect or section of audio or video material lasts.

edit—Any point on a magnetic tape where the audio or video information has been added to be replaced, or otherwise altered from its original form.

edit controller/editor—An electronic device assisting an operator (also called an editor) to make edits. Usually the device is electronically interfaced with the audio and/or video tape decks to control their motion and recording functions.

edit list (edit decision list, EDL)—A record of all the edit decisions made for a video program (such as time codes of edit in-points and out-points, types of transitions, etc.) stored as digital data in computer memory, on floppy disk, on punched tape, or printed on paper.

edit point (edit-in, edit-out)—The beginning and ending points for a selected event within a program, usually denoted by time code.

event number—A number assigned by the editor to each edit event recorded in an EDL (edit decision list).

flat room—A room that has been acoustically designed and/or treated to reproduce equally all sound in the audible spectrum. For a room that is not acoustically flat, the audio monitoring system may be conditioned through equalization to make the room seem flat.

fill material—Presence, ambience, or background sounds.

Foley—Creating sound effects by watching the picture and duplicating the action or simulating the natural sounds.

frame—One complete TV scanning cycle (approximately 1/30th second); contains two *fields.*.

frame address—The hours/minutes/seconds/frame numbers assigned each video frame in time code video tape editing.

frame lock—Synchronization between house video and taped time code.

futz (phone futz)—Electronic alteration of audio character, usually of dialog, through EQ, distortion, and addition of noise to simulate the sound heard through a telephone.

general-purpose interface (GPI)—An output from an edit controller or synchronizer used to trigger single events, e.g., to start or stop tape decks or to trigger electronic events.

graphic equalization—A type of audio signal processing which applies variable amplification or attenuation to an audio signal in fixed frequency bands. The amplification gain, cut or boost, may be independently adjusted for each frequency band.

hardware—The physical components (computer, cables, monitor, tape machine, etc.) that comprise an editing or video system.

high-pass filter—A device, usually electronic, which allows sounds or signals above a specified frequency to pass through, while suppressing those below the frequency threshold.

in-point—The beginning of an edit; the first frame that is recorded, denoted by time code.

intelligent interface—A sophisticated microprocessor-based controller of video and audio tape machines and switchers which receives commands from and communicates data to the main edit controller or computer.

interlock—The state of synchronous operation of two separate machines, achieved by a synchronizer by electronically comparing the time code from the two machines and adjusting speed until they are "locked together."

lavalier—A type of microphone characterized by small physical size , usually used to mic a speaking individual.

layback—Rerecording the sweetened, mixed audio track back to the edited master videotape, in sync.

laydown—The process of recording the audio track edited during the video edit from the edited master to the multitrack ATR.

level—A quantitative measure of either a video or an audio signal. A low level indicates the darker portions in video and the soft or quieter portions in audio; conversely, a high level indicates a brighter video image or a louder audio signal. Level of audio signal correlates directly with volume of reproduced sound.

LED—Light-emitting diode.

longitudinal time code (LTC)—Time code information encoded as an audio-like signal and recorded on audio channels of video or audio tape.

looping—Replacment of dialog in postproduction, in a way functionally similar to ADR, derived from earlier film processes using loops of film and magnetic film stock.

low-pass filter—A device, usually electronic, which allows sounds or signals below a specified frequency to pass through while suppressing those above the frequency threshold.

mag track—Magnetic recording tape fabricated in a physical format like film with sprocket holes for synchronization, used to record audio for film. A mag track is recorded and played on a mag film recorder or dubbing unit; each mag track is functionally equivalent to one audio track of a multitrack ATR.

master—In audio and video production, an original recording as differentiated from a copy or dub.

match-frame edit—An edit in which a scene already recorded on the master is continued with no apparent edit. Performed as a cut to the same source material at the frame which matches the previous out-point.

mixing console—An electronic device that adds, blends, and mixes various input signals in controllable ratios, usually with equalization. The mixed signals are sent out to other processing devices, monitoring systems, and ATRs.

monitor system—The amplifier and speakers or headphones used to listen to the audio in a control room or sweetening bay.

MOS—Recorded silent, or without sound; "mit out sound" in film folklore.

multitrack ATR—The audio tape recorder with 4, 8, 16, or more distinct channels onto which music, dialog, narration, and sound effects are recorded for audio sweetening.

murmur—A class of presence or ambient sound characteristic of the sound emanating from a crowd of people.

NAB—National Association of Broadcasters.

narration—Spoken explanation or story, usually over an accompanying visual of the subject being discussed.

noise—An unwanted signal mixed in with the desired signal. Noise is induced either acoustically, electronically, or magnetically in every stage of the recording/reproducing process.

non-drop frame—A convention for numbering frames in time code wherein every second has 30 frames. The result is that the time code differential of two points in a program is slightly greater than the actual elapsed clock time between the two points.

notch filter—A device, usually electronic, which suppresses signals in a fixed frequency band; signals above or below the limits of the band are passed through. Used to eliminate specific sounds of a particular frequency range.

NTSC format—A system of coding color information for television used primarily in the United States and Japan, formulated by the National Television Systems Committee in the early 1950s.

off-line editing—Editing that is done to produce an edit decision list, which is later used for assembling the program master with a computer assisted editing system. A reference tape, sometimes called a *work edit,* can be produced as a by-product of off-line editing.

on-line editing—Editing where the product is a finished program master.

pan pot—A continuously variable control for proportionately distributing one input to two buses or outputs. At opposite extremes the pan pot directs the input at maximum level to one of the buses; turning the pot in one direction decreases the level of input signal sent to one bus and increases the level sent to the other.

PAP system—An audio processing system invented by Glen Glenn Sound utilizing synchronized VTRs and ATRs for building the elements and the tracks which are mixed to complete a sweetened program. (The PAP abbreviation is usually taken to mean "post audio processing," though there is some disagreement among the originators on this point.)

parametric equalization—A type of audio signal processing which applies variable amplification or attenuation to an audio signal at selectable frequencies. The center frequency, the magnitude,and sometimes the bandwidth of the applied cut or boost processing are controllable.

phumpha—A garbled line or word in dialog resulting in an unintelligible sound.

pink noise—Random noise with a frequency spectrumn contoured such that to the human auditory perception system the noise appears flat across the audible spectrum.

ping-ponging—A process of recording, mixing, recording, remixing, back and forth among limited tracks of an ATR.

preroll—The number of frames between the cue point and the edit point; the minimum preroll is the time required for all machines in an edit to achieve sync or lock.

presence—Same as fill, ambience, or background sound. The natural noise level of a room or environment without dialog or other produced sounds, also called "room tone." Presence is used for filling holes created during editing, or under MOS footage.

punching in, punching out—Activating the record function of an ATR for selected channels, usually on the fly, i.e., as the ATR is running in sync with the source deck(s).

reader/punch—A combination machine consisting of both a tape punch (or perforator) and a tape reader.

reel number—The number assigned by the operator to each reel or cassette of video or audio tape used in an editing session.

rutabaga—To artificially create crowd murmur, five people stand around an open mic and recite at low volume, "Rutabaga, rutabaga, rutabaga . . ."

serial data—Digital data sequentially presented upon or transferred over a single line.

servo—A mechanical or electromechanical control system wherein performance charactistics are regulated through comparison of an output measurement or feedback with an input reference.

software—In computer terminology, the instructions loaded into computer memory that direct its operations. In sweetening, the non-hardware elements that contribute to audio producing, e.g., music and sound effects libraries.

Sonex—A brand of acoustic insulating material used to absorb and thereby inhibit reflections of sound from solid objects.

source VTR—A video tape machine that has audio material required for the sweetening process, such as dialog, ambient sounds, presence, or sound effects.

sound effects (SFX)—Lifelike imitations or duplications of sounds such as rain, creaking doors, hoofbeats, etc., prerecorded or produced artificially as called for during motion picture production, radio, TV programs, etc.

split edit—A type of edit transition where either the audio or video of the source is delayed from being recorded for a given time beyond the edit in-point of the other component.

spotting—The process of notating cues for music, narration, sound effects, etc., for the sweetening process.

SMPTE—Society of Motion Picture and Television Engineers.

SMPTE time code—See *time code.*

snivit—An incomplete sound usually created by an incorrect edit point. For example, if an edit should end at the end of a sentence of dialog, but the punch-out is a few frames late and the first syllable of the first word in the next sentence is recorded, that's a snivit.

sweeten—To make sweet to the taste; to make pleasing to the mind or senses; to increase the agreeable qualities.

sync—Pulses included in the video signal which provide a synchronizing reference for each frame and scanning line of the picture.

synchronization—The precise coincidence of two signals, pulses, or events. In sweetening, two or more ATRs or VTRs playing precisely matched material at precisely the same speed.

synchronizer—The microprocessor-controlled device that reads time code from both the VTR and ATR and interlocks the two (or more) machines in perfect synchronization. Other functions include record trigger, multiple source triggers, etc.

three-stripe—A convention used in film audio of producing three distinct sound tracks for dialog, music, and effects.

time code—A standardized numeric coding convention, both logical and electronic, used to uniquely identify segments of video by numerically labeling each sequential frame; analogously used in audio. Frame numbering follows drop or non-drop frame conventions.

trim—To add or subtract from an edit in-point, out-point, or duration, quantified in frames or time code.

U-Matic—Identifies the standard 3/4″ video cassette recording medium-physical specification of cassette, motion characteristics, electronic and magnetic recording format, etc.

upcut—Loss of the beginning of an audio source, for example if an edit in-point is slightly late and the first syllable of dialog is cut off so the sentence begins in the middle of a word.

user bits—Undefined bits in the 80-bit SMPTE time code word that are available for uses other than time code.

vertical interval time code (VITC)—Time code for video, following the SMPTE digital numeric convention, encoded into a composite video signal in the vertical interval.

video cassette—Video tape prepackaged in self-enclosed plastic cassettes, e.g., 3/4″ U-matic, 1/2″ VHS or 1/2″ Beta; any or all may be involved in sweetening.

VCR—Video cassette recorder.

white noise—For audio purposes, random sound with an even or flat distribution of frequencies within the audio spectrum.

Index

Index

Edited by Stephen Moore